Aligned Influence®: Beyond Governance

ADVANCE PRAISE

Ken Schuetz's book *Aligned Influence: Beyond Governance* absolutely nails it! The Aligned Influence process gives boards and executives a clear approach for effectively collaborating, leading, managing, and genuinely benefiting their organization. I highly recommend this book. It's a must-read.

—**Bruce Beck**, president and founder of The Essentials Group, LLC, author of *The Essentials of Leadership*, and former executive at Eli Lilly and Company

Those who are selected for governing body service must hit the ground running, juggling multiple priorities and conflicting demands even as they find their bearings on their new team. Aligned Influence is the governance model for those who need an efficient ramp-up to maximum organizational effectiveness but don't have a whole year to get there. The Aligned Influence model is a sensible, streamlined, and practical approach to defining the work of an organization's governing body and its CEO, and then aligning their respective spheres of responsibility towards the accomplishment of the organization's mission and goals. *Aligned Influence: Beyond Governance* explains this new model and shows how effective it can be.

—**Tami Tanoue**, Attorney

From the work floors right on up to the C-suites and the board-room, contention is a company killer. Because organizational cultures are rife with strife, leaders have leveraged politics and power time and again for personal gain, flinging for-profits and non-profits off the path of their mission. It's time for change-oriented leaders to take up *Aligned Influence: Beyond Governance* by Ken Schuetz. With keen insights drawn from years of experience, Ken has pioneered a path forward for boards and executives that goes beyond current governance models and provides the way to clear and sensible organizational alignment. Applying Aligned Influence, organizations can finally make big wins while encouraging healthy discourse and collaboration over destructive competitions for power and influence within.

> **—Jennifer Hayden Epperson, EdD** (organizational leadership), author, educator, and radio professional

In *Aligned Influence: Beyond Governance*, Ken Schuetz presents a simple six-word model that illustrates fundamental roles for boards and executives. Resources are always limited. When change and financial challenge impact an organization, it is simple truths and principles that should define resource priorities. What Ken does well is avoid the traditional legal perspective. Rather, he presents a board and management model structured around getting to the ideal outcome for the organization. His approach not only focuses on simple truths, it also connects them with structure and easily understood practice. *Aligned Influence* is a great read, and it's especially important for board and management leaders, assurance providers, and regulators.

> **—Daniel Clayton, CPA, CIA, CKM**; management consultant; accountability consulting; author of *Sawyer's Internal Auditing: Enhancing and Protecting Organizational Value*, 7th edition

Protecting the organization from cyber security threats has been a top priority for chief information officers (CIOs) in most organizations for the past decade, and the trend continues. In an ever-expanding technology landscape, it is challenging at best to keep up with the sophistication and speed of the latest attacks. As a cyber security consultant working with different organizations and in many industries, I often find that boards of directors and executives lack an understanding of the threats, their adversaries, and the role they have in determining the actions necessary to mitigate the risks. This may result in inaction or suboptimal use of resources, and it can exacerbate the risks. The Aligned Influence model equips these important stakeholders with a framework to effectively tackle the challenges. Through complimentary roles and purposeful dialog about cyber security risk, it is possible to gain a shared understanding of the top cyber security concerns, the impacts to the business, and determine the best possible mitigation approaches. Ken Schuetz's book, *Aligned Influence: Beyond Governance*, presents this critically important approach.

—**Stig Ravdal**, president, Ravdal Inc., cyber security

As an expert in the employee experience, measuring the alignment and effectiveness of boards of directors and executive teams has been a "missing link" in our industry. Ken Schuetz and Aligned Influence have provided a framework that has allowed us, in partnership, to create a robust assessment tool that finally addresses this need, leading to much needed insight and clarity to further strengthen organizational leadership and governance. Ken's book, *Aligned Influence: Beyond Governance*, unpacks the essentials of this framework, providing leaders with critical structure, strength, and enrichment for their organizations in today's complex environment.

—**Leanne Buehler, PhD**, managing partner and vice president of Consulting Services, Newmeasures, LLC

As the executive director for an association of forty colleges and schools, I'm keenly aware of the critical relationship that exists between boards and the leaders they select to steward their organizations. When this relationship is healthy and both understand and execute their respective roles, the organization flourishes. But when the relationship is uninformed or troubled, so is the organization. Ken Schuetz's book, *Aligned Influence: Beyond Governance*, represents a treasure trove of valuable insights for boards and organizational leaders, providing a clear pathway to organizational success. I've worked with Ken personally and witnessed the impressive results of his Aligned Influence model firsthand. *Aligned Influence: Beyond Governance* is a must-read for any organization seeking to enhance its effectiveness.

—**Colonel Ray Rottman**, USAF (ret), executive director of Association of Military Colleges and Schools of the United States

As a leader of an organization who is trying to help more people, my primary concern is expanding our capacity. Since we adopted the Aligned Influence model, we've been able to quadruple the number of families served. What makes this model unique is its ability to leverage different perspectives and channel those individual energies in a complementary way. Our ministry has no fewer than eight distinct groups of stakeholders. Each group has a unique perspective, and each plays a critical role. Using this model, those stakeholders each contribute in a way that magnifies the efforts of the others. *Aligned Influence: Beyond Governance* articulates this model so any organization can benefit from it.

—**David C. Emerson**, executive director, Habitat for Humanity of the St. Vrain Valley, Colorado

The Aligned Influence model for aligning the roles of our heads of schools and their boards of directors and the associated development processes have proven to be a valuable resource for our member schools. I highly recommend that you consider taking advantage of the *Aligned Influence* book, and the services and consulting work that Ken Schuetz and his associates will provide to your school!

—**David M. Ray**, assistant vice president,
Strategic Partners/Student Services,
Association of Christian Schools International

I inherited a board that was stable but struggling with how to grow to serve more of the community. The concepts in *Aligned Influence: Beyond Governance* have helped our board and executive to define their roles so that we can focus on the future. As a board chairperson, I can say that I finally understand my role in a way that allows me to be an ally of the executive director and still provide the needed checks and balances that are required of our board. In this book, Ken Schuetz will provide all of my peer chairpersons with the same clarity.

—**Brett Lundy**, president of the board of directors,
Coastal Empire Habitat for Humanity

ALIGNED INFLUENCE®
BEYOND GOVERNANCE

A BETTER WAY FORWARD
FOR BOARDS, EXECUTIVES,
AND THEIR ORGANIZATIONS

KEN SCHUETZ

NEW YORK

LONDON • NASHVILLE • MELBOURNE • VANCOUVER

Aligned Influence®: Beyond Governance

A Better Way Forward for Boards, Executives, and Their Organizations

Published in New York, New York, by Morgan James Publishing. Morgan James is a trademark of Morgan James, LLC. www.MorganJamesPublishing.com

Aligned Influence is a trademark of Aligned Influence, LLC. www.AlignedInfluence.com

ISBN 9781631951749 paperback
ISBN 9781631951756 eBook
Library of Congress Control Number: 2020937674

Cover Design by:
Christopher Kirk
www.GFSstudio.com

Interior Design by:
Chris Treccani
www.3dogcreative.net

Morgan James is a proud partner of Habitat for Humanity Peninsula and Greater Williamsburg. Partners in building since 2006.

Get involved today! Visit
MorganJamesPublishing.com/giving-back

CONTENTS

FOREWORD

I first encountered Ken Schuetz and his Aligned Influence® model several years ago. At the time, I was a director of strategy for the University of Texas System Audit Office. My role was focused on identifying the best models and ideas in governance, risk management, and internal control, and then finding opportunities to improve internal audit deliverables. This means I am a student and avid researcher of good governance practices. I have collected hundreds of digital and print resources on governance. However, it was not until 2017 when I was asked to consult on improving processes for developing regent rules and policies that I was truly able to see the beauty in Ken's simple approach.

Many books out there on governance for board members, auditors, and regulators begin with assumptions about leading practices and then offer some additional incremental value. In this book, *Aligned Influence: Beyond Governance*, Ken seeks a new level of transformational value, and he illustrates his unique ability to think deeper and challenge historical paradigms. I see his mission for Aligned Influence and this publication as an effort to increase harmony between boards and management as they address growing complexities and the challenges of perpetual change. This work will not only help the board and executive team, it is also relevant to assurance providers and regulators seeking to efficiently and effectively increase positive organizational outcomes. Why? Because the Aligned Influence approach is simple and true, and it structures governance goals in a way neatly tied to the desired mission and outcomes of an organization.

The world is changing, and that change is accelerating. Tomorrow's leaders will need to keep up. Not only will they need to know how to stage perpetual change, they must also manage growing complexity and the drive to create bigger and bigger interdependent systems. However, such systems cannot be created without shared purpose, shared definitions, and shared understanding. Yet when one asks a simple question like "What is good Governance?," they find a few standards and many opinions. Most of those responses rest on the legal requirements of a board. But when we begin with a legal perspective, we risk eliminating, or at least weakening, the connection of board activities to the desired organizational outcomes. Ken eliminates this risk with an insightful and revolutionary model that he captures in six simple words: boards *direct*, *protect*, and *enable*, and executives *lead*, *manage*, and *accomplish*.

I was able to use these simple words to develop new expectations for the development of regent rules and policies that directly promoted mission success and eliminated unnecessary legalese and legal process influence. I also identified imbalance where rules that directed without enabling created internal conflict.

What Ken offers in this book is a way to look at the core of good governance. It is a first and essential step in defining governance structures that can endure perpetual change and create principles that are more capable of becoming commodities in large interdependent systems. This book fills important gaps in connecting what a board does directly to the mission and the value they want to achieve.

Daniel Clayton, CPA, CIA, CKM
Consultant and author of *Sawyer's Internal Auditing: Enhancing and Protecting Organizational Value*, 7th edition

1

A Revolution in Governance and Beyond

Today we take for granted that the sun is the center of our solar system and that the other planets, including our own, circle around that burning star. But what we assume true today—and have established even more thoroughly since the idea was first proposed—was not the prevailing view for a long time in human history.

In the second century, Egyptian astronomer, mathematician, and geographer Ptolemy argued that the earth was stationary and that the sun and other planets revolved around our planet. His view—the geocentric model—became the standard understanding for more than a thousand years. During that time, various problems surfaced with his theory and a number of fixes were offered, but all of them just made the geocentric model more complicated and none of them resolved all of its inherent difficulties.

Then, in the first half of the 1500s, Polish astronomer and mathematician Copernicus calculated that all the difficulties with Ptolemy's view could be solved with one clear yet huge change:

treat the sun as the unmoved center, with the earth and the other planets revolving around this light-giving heavenly body.

When Copernicus first published his heliocentric view of our solar system, he knew he was proposing a radical break from Ptolemy's paradigm. And yet he expressed his admiration for Ptolemy and his work and regarded himself as following in Ptolemy's footsteps. While Copernicus's heliocentric model took time to take hold and receive the verification it needed to supplant Ptolemy's geocentric model, the shift significantly and forever altered astronomy. The field would never be the same. A true revolution had occurred in science.

Of course, like Copernicus, Ptolemy did not work in a vacuum. Many ancient peoples before him, including the Egyptians, Babylonians, Hebrews, and Greeks, had made numerous observations about the heavenlies and drawn a host of inferences from what they witnessed. Ptolemy learned from them while putting forward his own views, which, in many ways, advanced astronomy, mathematics, and map-making far beyond what his predecessors had accomplished. Likewise, Copernicus was able to make the advance he did because of what Ptolemy and his successors had done. Just as Ptolemy stood on the shoulders of the work of others, so did Copernicus.

What's true in science is also true in all other fields of human endeavor, including in organizational development and governance. If you work in a place that has a board and a lead executive, you are in an organizational model that has a rich and varied past. Your workplace may be just a few years old or even just months old, but that its oversight relies, in part, on a board is far older.

In fact, legal scholar Franklin Gevurtz traces the beginnings of boards back to the fifteenth and sixteenth centuries in European guilds. But the conceptual norms on which these guilds established their boards have roots going back centuries earlier to ancient Roman ideas of republican rule, some old Germanic traditions, and medieval Christian ideas of community as practiced by church organizations, especially church councils.[1] In other words, organizations with the complexity of a board have been around a very long time. And the foundations on which they were built are even older. Furthermore, attempts to improve organizational structure, procedures, governance, and the like, have been ongoing during that entire time.

History shows that none of us thinks, theorizes, creates, invents, or works in any other ways without building on the labor of countless others who have gone before us. We may not always realize how dependent our work is on those who preceded us, but this doesn't negate the truth of our reliance on others.

I am no different. I am indebted to Policy Governance creator John Carver and many others who have worked on board governance, organizational structure and development, leadership, and the many other matters I discuss in this book. I have read my predecessors, listened to them, learned from them, and even built upon many of their ideas and processes in my own work. But just as Copernicus found a way forward that challenged and improved upon Ptolemy's astronomical model, I believe I have found a much better way forward with boards, executives, and organizational alignment and development. My approach, Aligned Influence, came out of my attempt to solve the problems resident in the other models. I was determined to find a better way forward for organizations and their governance.

Origins of Aligned Influence

In 2011, I retired from a thirty-plus-year stint serving as an executive in higher education. During that time, I worked alongside scholars in a wide variety of disciplines, led dozens of employees at any one time, and worked with a number of fellow executives. I prepared reports that were used for review by boards of directors, and I served on boards in and outside the field of education. By the time I retired, I had a desire to help boards learn how to better lead and serve their respective organizations. I thought I knew many of the right answers for doing this, and decided I could fill in the remaining blanks using Carver's Policy Governance model.[2] His was the board model I found used most often, and it seemed to present all the right answers. So I steeped myself in his model and began to use it in my work with organizations.

It did not take long, however, before I began to see shortcomings in his approach. While in many respects Carver has done a real service for board development and function, his model's strengths are also its weaknesses. Simply solving many issues with boards, which Carver's approach does, still doesn't translate into organizational improvement. Addressing a part of the problem doesn't handle the whole problem. More was needed. But what was the *more*?

I conveyed my struggles with Policy Governance in a variety of conversations with individuals who worked in for-profit and non-profit settings. I started asking questions—basic, essential questions—about leadership, organizations, organizational structure, relational and vocational dynamics, and on the list went. These questions led to more questions. Fortunately, in time, bit by bit, insight by insight, answers started coming—answers that often surprised me yet fit the facts so much better than the "answers" I had previously accepted.

Many of the individuals I talked to encouraged me to put my discoveries into writing and through that to start finding and developing my voice to speak into the current discussion about organizational leadership, structure, and the like. At first this writing took the form of "white papers." These were brief articulations of my developing positions on boards and executives, and on organizational leadership and structure.[3]

Through this writing process as well as my work with a large number of boards and their organizations, I developed a new approach to organizational leadership and structure. I call this model Aligned Influence. I have presented it to the boards, executives, and staffs of numerous organizations—organizations as diverse as businesses and charities, civic governing bodies and educational institutions, churches and foundations, sports enterprises, military institutes, and law offices. I have walked them through the implementation of Aligned Influence, and have seen how well it works. Even in organizations that were once dedicated to Policy Governance, my Aligned Influence model has found new and avid advocates.

I entered into this domain out of a desire to help organizations improve. I had no idea when I began that I would end up developing an approach that I now know—and am demonstrating—is much better than the other models currently available. I have had the privilege and opportunity to not just theorize about Aligned Influence but also apply it and prove its effectiveness.

Aligned Influence vs. Other Models

One of my clients said in an interview, "The one area that I think we were somewhat lacking [before adopting Aligned Influence] is there was confusion between the staff and the board and perhaps some disagreement in regard to what role the board played or did not play in regard to high level resource development and advocacy." But after adopting Aligned Influence and reaping its benefits for several years, he reflected, "We were growing before we looked at Aligned Influence, but that has only increased [since implementing Aligned Influence]. We're now active in almost double the amount of places that we were working. We've doubled the types of services and nearly quadrupled the amount of families that we're serving."[4] Aligned Influence made an already successful organization even more effective. Aligned Influence makes a difference—a difference that matters, a difference that no other governance model provides.

Policy Governance, for example, moves boards toward compliance with existing law. Aligned Influencedoes this too, but it doesn't stop there. Rather it moves boards, executives, *and* their organizations toward effectiveness through alignment between their board and executives and the rest of the organization's staff.

No current governance model is holistic. All of them seek to address parts of the organizational whole. Aligned Influence, however, deals with the organizational parts in light of the whole ecosystem of influence. It is a holistic approach from top to bottom.

None of the current approaches to governance bring simplicity and clarity to board roles and executive roles. But Aligned Influence does both through just six words: three that apply to boards and three that apply to executives. And these words express and summarize the vertical relationship of roles within the board and within the chief executive and her team, and as pairs these words reveal the alignment of roles between board members and executives.

The key problem with all the solutions offered for boards and executives is the problem of alignment. Rather than tackling this problem head-on with truly viable solutions, the world of organizational governance has tried to rely on establishing written policies, saying that we just need the right policies to solve existing problems.

Policies, however, are tools; they are not solutions. They help us set up the legal framework for an organization and they document solutions, but they are not the solutions we need for a comprehensive approach to organizational governance. They may satisfy the legal department, but beyond that they will not help. Attorneys tend to see governance as a legal issue, so they insist that organizations must have the bylaws in place. Legally, this is true and necessary. But once the necessary policies are laid out, what then? An organization must develop, grow, and succeed. And that requires dealing with such matters as the way power is shared in the organization, and seeing that this is important for organizational sustainability over time. The legal framework can help establish an organization, but it will not help the organization grow in its capacity.

Consider: Is governance a legal or a development issue? In reality, it's both. Policies and law address the legal side of governance but not the development side. Legally, the government says you must have a board. So by putting certain policy sets in place that conform to the law, your organization convinces the government that it understands what the board's role and organization's role are at a very high level: you're going to have officers and you're going to meet at certain times of the year, here's how you're going to bring officers on the board, and so on. Beyond these legal requirements, what do you do now? Policy sets won't give you the answers you need.

Aligned Influence incorporates the value that policy sets supply while going far beyond them. Aligned Influence provides legal compliance while recognizing that governance and organizational effectiveness require much more. And it is this *more* that Aligned Influence supplies.

None of the existing models provide an effective solution for the wide array of conflicts of interest and competition that inevitably arise in human enterprises. Aligned Influence lays out an approach that addresses these all-too-common problems for all the influencers in an organization, not just those who meet in the boardroom or executive offices.

Unlike all of the other governance models, Aligned Influence recognizes and takes seriously the fact that alignment always comes before effectiveness. The "solutions" the other approaches offer work around the alignment issue without solving it. Aligned Influence drives to the center of the alignment need and addresses it in a holistic way.

Every organization needs a board if it is managing someone else's money. So for-profits and nonprofits need boards. Civic organizations do as well. They have councils or trustees because they also are managing someone else's money (that of taxpayers). In the *for-profit* world, organizations tried to get rid of the alignment problem and protect investor dollars by having the chief executive on the board. This allowed for and even led to money-making, but it failed to solve the alignment problem and it failed to protect investors. The *nonprofit* approach to managing funds led to policy creation, but it too failed to adequately address the critical relational alignment between the operating arm of the executive and the overseeing role of the board, and it did not ensure that donor dollars would be used as intended.

Moreover, in nonprofit and for-profit organizations, board members and executives generally know what the policies are, but they are not sure what they should do once legal compliance is achieved: How do I support you? How do I lead you or the organization? This situation has created power struggles: Who's really in charge? Who really holds the future of the organization? Who holds whom accountable to make sure we are doing the right things? And legal compliance is inadequate to answer the question, What should I do now?

Carver, through his Policy Governance model, tried to solve these problems by saying that the executive is in charge and the board should establish policies and review compliance to those policies while not looking around the curtain to the side of the executive, much like the Wizard of Oz kept many of his activities hidden behind a large curtain barrier. Carver tried to solve the alignment problem by artificially limiting it to policies and legal compliance. But this has failed to bring the alignment so critical to organizational development.

Aligned Influence, on the other hand, speaks directly to boards, executives, and the entire ecosystem of influence in organizations. No one is left out. Roles are clearly defined, known, and aligned while policies are established that not only bring compliance but also support alignment. And vital conversations are encouraged at all levels of the organization, not just at the top. As one of my clients said:

> What I think was really unique about the experience with Ken [and his Aligned Influence approach] was that you were able to take a conversation, which is a hard conversation, and frame it in a way where it's safe to have that conversation and it's productive to have that conversation. . . . I think the best part was that . . . there was a framework where staff and our town clerk could have a real conver-

sation, an honest conversation, about roles, about frustrations, and it was really productive for us.[5]

The Promise of Aligned Influence

The promise of Aligned Influence is huge:

- It brings an end to destructive competitions for power and conflicts of interest.
- Board members finally know what they should do and why.
- It gives boards the to-do role of enablement that no other governance model provides.
- Executives are freed to do the organization's work, knowing how the board supports them.
- Leadership roles are clearly defined and genuinely aligned.
- Alignment from the top down gives everyone within the organization a strong sense that their organization is well governed and has a clear vision, and that each person knows his or her role within the whole.
- With what I call the "ecosystem of influence" acknowledged and sufficiently addressed, internal resources of creativity, leadership, ingenuity, and so many other talents and skills are unleashed and rightly channeled for the organization's benefit and that of its investors and stakeholders.
- It provides a clear and essential framework for structural health in an organization.
- It lays the groundwork for organizational effectiveness and sustainability.
- Through organizational health, productivity grows at a faster, more reliable pace.
- Investor and donor dollars are protected.

- Stakeholders feel more secure about the organization's ongoing viability and vitality.
- The organization remains structurally healthy even if proven and profitable leaders move on.

I could keep adding benefits that Aligned Influence brings, but these listed are enough to establish that this model stands alone in its ability to deliver on what the other governance models simply cannot do. In short, Aligned Influence is bringing about a Copernican-like revolution in organizational governance.

This is a bold claim, I know. When I began this venture, I knew I was on to something. How big it was, I did not immediately grasp. I only knew that I was finding uncommon and beneficial solutions to governance problems. The more insight I gained, the better the Aligned Influence model became. And the more difference it made, the more I found myself thinking of Copernicus and wondering how long it took him to realize the full significance of the solution he proposed.

Only time will tell all that organizations will be able to accomplish through the Aligned Influence framework. But that it is a much better way forward, I have no doubt. The rest of this book is about this new way: why it is needed, what comprises it, what it can accomplish, the general steps for implementing it, and the types of organizations it can benefit.

PART I

The Need for Something Better

2

Alignment Matters

Figure 1

W hat's wrong with this picture?

Two gears sitting side by side, not connected to each other, much less to anything else.

When I show this image to board members and executives, some think the gears have the ability to go in different directions and at different speeds. If there are engineers in the group, they see a machine that can't do any work because there's no way for disconnected gears to transfer power from one to the other. No power, no work, nothing accomplished.

Now, imagine under the left gear the label *Board* and under the right gear the label *Executive Team*. When board members and executives think about this image with these labels, the conversation changes. Some members from both leadership sides often indicate that they feel successful in their respective roles but not when they engage those on the other side of the leadership spectrum. Feelings of frustration usually emerge. Board members and executives alike don't understand why their good intentions don't get them to where they want to be. A united sense of success is elusive. And when success does happen, it seems to be more by accident than by design.

With this situation in mind, executives ask, "How can we be successful with our current board of directors?" Board members ask, "How can we work more successfully with our current executive director and her team?" And executives and board members ask, "How can we be more effective together?"

When I ask what answers they have heard to their questions, I get the typical old and tired "answers":

1. "It's all about managing the personalities on your board or executive team." So the solution to the misalignment between boards and executives is for each side to have a better psychological handle on who they are dealing with. This may require greater sensitivity toward one another, relationship building, more sharing times, and the like. Or maybe we need to require that everyone take various personality tests so we can type each person and use the results to hone our abilities to better connect with them and mo-

tivate them. Of course, organizations have engaged in these activities for many years, and yet the misalignments persist.

2. "It's all about controlling who is on your board or executive team." With this answer, the solution lies with the selection process. If we just had the right people in leadership, all would be well. While the selection process and result are valuable, once the individuals are there to fill the leadership positions, they still need to know what to do and how to do it. And board members still need to know how to work with executives, and executives still need to know how to work with board members. The selection choice is not enough to solve the misalignment problem.

3. "It's all about the board or executive team understanding their respective roles." This is critically important, but on its own, it too is an inadequate answer. What are those roles, and how should they be aligned? The misaligned gears illustration assumes that boards and executives have some sense about what they should do with their time. What it also reveals is that this understanding is insufficient to align boards and executives so they actually function together properly and efficiently.

4. "It's all about getting the right executive director." While similar to answer two, this answer focuses just on the executive side of the organization. But what constitutes the "right" person for this job? Doesn't that depend on what the executive's role is and how this person is supposed to

relate to and rely upon the board and vice versa? This puts us back to the alignment issue. What the board and chief executive are supposed to do and how their roles align have to be defined independently of who serves as the chief executive. In fact, an organization will not genuinely know they have found the "right" person to be their chief executive until they resolve the disconnection issue at the top.

The reality is that, for an organization that has the complexity of a board of directors and an executive team, a significant disconnect between them leads to a host of problems. I call this disconnect misalignment.

As a consultant who frequently meets with board members, I often hear signs of misalignment in comments such as these:

- "I don't know why I'm here on the board."
- "I don't understand what I'm supposed to be doing."
- "I don't know how I'm supposed to make the organization better."
- "I feel like I'm wasting my time."
- "I feel like I'm here several times a year to get material from the executive, but beyond that there's nothing for me to do."
- "I didn't realize I was expected to solve the challenges we are facing as an organization."
- "I feel like I keep getting drawn into operational issues, but I don't think this is supposed to happen. Is this a problem? I just don't know."

Notice how there's a lack of known purpose ("I don't know why I'm here"), a lack of understanding the board's role ("I don't understand what I'm supposed to be doing" and "I don't know how I am supposed to make the organization better"), feelings of futility ("I feel like I'm wasting my time"), no real to-do role beyond reviewing reports ("I feel like I'm here several times a year to get material from the executive, but beyond that there's nothing for me to do"), unstated expectations ("I didn't realize I was expected to solve the challenges we are facing"), and role confusion ("I feel like I keep getting drawn into operational issues, but I don't think this is supposed to happen"). And these represent problems that are more readily sensed and observed. All too frequently, board members don't have in their purview the larger organizational consequences that too often flow from misalignment.

In my time with board members, I've found that many of them feel lost; they're wandering around the organizational desert and mountain passes with little to no direction and no clear sense of purpose. Misalignment at the board level benefits no one, and it leaves organizations unprotected and poorly directed.

As bad as all of this is, it's not just board members who experience misalignment. Executives do as well. Here are some of the comments I typically hear:

- "I feel like I'm constantly defending myself before the board."
- "I feel like I'm in this work alone; it's all up to me."
- "I feel as if the board is in my way; I can't make any progress because the board is holding me back."
- "I'm so busy making sure the board is operating that I don't have time to run the organization."

A lack of support ("I feel like I'm constantly defending myself before the board" and "I feel like I'm in this work alone"), role confusion and competitions for power ("I feel like the board is in my way; I can't make any progress because the board is holding me back"), a lack of clearly identified roles and responsibilities ("I'm so busy making sure the board is operating that I don't have time to run the organization")—these are just some of the signs from the executive side that the board–executive relationship is out of alignment and harming the work of the organization. If left unresolved, such alignment problems can foster innumerable other issues, including executives leaving, disgruntled staff, and loss of investor confidence.

Misalignment matters regardless of whether one's organization is for-profit or nonprofit, small or large, secular or faith based, a start-up or seasoned, national or international. If the board and executive team are misaligned, they will harm and even undermine their organization's direction, operation, leadership, management, effectiveness, and sustainability.

One way I like to surface this alignment problem is to ask board members and executives the same question: "Who is leading your organization?" The response has become predictable. I first see a puzzled look and then comes the comment, "That's a trick question, isn't it? We both lead the organization, don't we?" My response is always, "You're probably right. How is that working for *both* of you to lead the organization?"

From here the conversation is off and running. My question brings immediate clarity to the alignment problem they are facing. It unearths issues lurking beneath the surface: issues concerning competitions for power and influence, conflicting understandings of roles and responsibilities, personality clashes, differences over the direction and commitments of the organization, and a host of other issues that can derail even the best intentions, plans, and skill sets.

Are your board and executive team connected in your organization? Are they functioning together in productive ways?

Or, like the gears above, are they disconnected? Maybe at odds with each other? Creating more harm than good? Or perhaps as they turn independently of each other, they are wondering why their hard work is not making the difference in the organization that they expected it would. Unable to properly transfer influence from one side to the other, they find themselves frustrated, struggling to bring to their organization all the positive benefits they seek.

If your organization's leadership gears are out of sync, your organization is in trouble—and so are its investors and stakeholders. Let's start with some examples from the nonprofit sector and then move to the for-profit one.

Alignment Problems
In Nonprofits

I worked with a private school that had served its community for about twenty years. It had slowly yet steadily grown over time but within the context of the local church with which it was connected. The school was, in fact, a ministry of the church, but it had started to outgrow the church that had supported it and even housed it. In size, vision, and other ways, the school was starting to exceed what its host could accommodate.

The school had a group they called a board, but this board began to realize there were some things they didn't know when it came to thinking about what their role was. They found that their role was not well defined, so they were confused about what they should be doing and how. And now that the school had a new head administrator who wanted to move the school forward, the board found itself ill prepared to assess where she wanted to go and why, much less how it could move with her. The leadership gears between the board and the executive were clearly misaligned.

I also worked with a church that had the same senior pastor for twenty-five years. With that pastor, the church had experienced growth from a couple of hundred to close to nine hundred attendees. Like many churches, the senior pastor did almost everything: he set direction for the church and led it in virtually every other way, including managing its various activities, including its staff, and quietly dealing with issues that surfaced so they would not hurt the church and its ministry.

When the senior pastor decided to retire, the other leaders saw that the church was going to be in crisis. While the church had a board, it was incapable of guiding the church through a transition of leadership. The pastor had been the one to provide the essential oversight of the church and to lead it and manage it. The church board, however, had limited itself to praying for the sick, providing discipline of members when necessary (which was rare), and performing other "oversight" roles they had discerned from their understanding of key Bible texts. But little of what they did actually fulfilled essential oversight, direction-setting tasks. In effect, they were a board largely in name only. They had left the most important leadership tasks to the senior pastor, who had now announced that he was on his way out. Without him, they didn't know what to do.

The church had succeeded because it had a pastor who was a super-person—providing leadership and basically working without genuine oversight. The conservative positions and roles of the church had kept it far away from the borders of trouble. And it had been fortunate enough to have not experienced some serious failure at the leadership level. But the board didn't understand how their role connected to that of the pastor. The pastor and board were two different gears disconnected from each other. Now the board had to figure out how to move forward with the most important leader leaving the church.

In still another case, I came across a nonprofit that for many years had operated with a board of directors that thought they needed to be involved in the details of the day-to-day operations of their organization. Although the organization had experienced some growth for several years, the board was now faced with a huge opportunity to go to the next level of what they could do for the community they lived and worked in.

The problem, however, was that the board members realized they could not take advantage of this golden opportunity if they continued to help operate the organization. This situation frustrated the organization's executive. She wanted to accept the new challenge, but the board's heavy involvement in operations was now clearly hindering the organization's capacity to grow and advance. This board and executive realized that they needed to think differently about what their roles were and how they needed to be aligned. In this case, the organizational gears were misaligned, not because they were disconnected, operating in their own spheres, but because they severely overlapped, with the board doing the work of the organization rather than overseeing it (see chapter 2 for more on this misaligned approach).

Misalignment can have far more devastating impacts in nonprofit organizations than I have mentioned so far. For instance, in October 2013, CharityWatch highlighted a number of organizations as the worst perpetrators of a variety of corruption disorders, including theft, fraud, cover-ups, financial mismanagement, and the self-enrichment of their founders or other organizational leaders at the expense of the organizations they led.[6] In addition, the *Dallas Morning News* in April 2012 noted other nonprofit organizations that dealt with financial mismanagement in their own ranks, some of which led to significant changes at the boardroom level.[7] Add to these the sex scandals linked to numerous Roman Catholic and Protestant churches as well as parachurch organizations, and one can readily see that many nonprofits suffer from leadership and protection issues that undermine the public's confidence in them.

Misalignment matters, and it can occur in many ways. But the problem is not just found in nonprofits. It happens in for-profits as well.

In For-Profits

In the corporate world, the chief executive officer often sits as the chairperson on the board of directors. The gear of the executive virtually overlaps the gear of the board. In other words, the skills, responsibilities, and roles of the executive are duplicated by members of the board. Whatever the executive can do, the board can do. Whatever the board can do, the executive can do. The board and the executive are mirror images of one another.

Moreover, board members in the corporate world are often paid, and they are selected as people who have strong opinions about the operations of the organization. Board members who have been CFOs may want to see their approaches to finances and financial development enacted, while board members who have had ample success in marketing, sales, or distribution will want to speak into those areas and have their ideas put into effect by the executive team. The board's top-down approach to leadership is internally focused, centered on how the organization runs, when it should be more externally focused on protecting investors and engaging stakeholders (those who care that the organization exists).

This approach to organizational governance is so common in the for-profit world that many people don't even realize that it displays serious misalignment. At least two factors show this. One is that this governance approach provides fertile ground for conflicts of interest and competitions for power between the board and executive. After all, why do I need you if you can do what I do? And if you can duplicate me, why am I needed? In such an environment, how does each of us carve out distinctive roles and responsibilities without overstepping our boundaries? Indeed, where are the boundaries in such a situation? And if I struggle, you can simply step in and do my job or even remove me so you can have my job. How does that breed security? It doesn't. Instead it fosters self-protection and usually unhealthy acts of competition. Suspicion and turf protection abound at the top in the for-profit world.

This leads to the second sign of misalignment: self-protection at the top rather than investor protection, and a mutual desire to hide or misrepresent financial loss or mismanagement. Those at the top can become more concerned, even consumed, over making profits and protecting themselves or the organization they lead rather than looking out for those who invested their money and other resources into the organization. Investors suffer loss while those at the top often defend themselves and strive to shield themselves from damaging consequences. Boards and executives end up failing those they were supposed to protect. Their misalignment makes it easy for them to become internally focused and self-protective. Their external relationship to stockholders and stakeholders takes a back seat, at best. They may even come to see stockholders and stakeholders as nuisances to appease and keep at bay, even through misinformation if necessary.

We don't have to imagine the consequences of such an approach to governance. In the early part of the twenty-first century, it came to light that the leaders of numerous companies had failed their investors, employees, vendors, and even entire communities that were dependent on them. The *New York Times* in the summer of 2002 listed a number of these major American companies, noting in them the occurrence of damaging lapses in leadership involving auditing, insider trading, the inflation of revenue, and the hiding of loans or losses. In their book *Inside the Boardroom*, Richard Leblanc and James Gillies summarized the damage wrought by these companies (and numerous others):

> Retirees, employees, shareholders, bondholders, creditors and suppliers lost upwards of tens of millions and in some cases billions of dollars as a consequence of mismanagement, accounting fraud, false reporting and totally misleading, if not downright dishonest, investment advice. The investments and pension plans of literally thousands of individuals and families were "wiped out" or essentially rendered worthless as a result of the breakdown in the institutions of capitalism.[8]

As a consequence of these actions and their effects, then US President George W. Bush delivered a major speech addressing the issue of corporate responsibility. Among other things, he "outlined proposals for imposing strict discipline and punishment on corporate wrongdoers, and reiterated his administration's support for corporate governance reforms." Soon after this speech, the US Congress overwhelmingly passed the Public Company Accounting Reform and Investor Protection Act, which has come to be known as Sarbanes-Oxley, after the names of the legislators who drafted the bill. This legislation "called for broad new regulations, described as the most far-reaching in over seventy years, affecting issuers of publicly traded securities, corporate directors and independent advisers such as auditors and lawyers. The Act was signed by the President and enacted into law on July 30, 2002."[9]

This kind of governmental reach into the public marketplace is nothing new. For example, during the 1700s and through the mid 1800s, sectors of the American marketplace willingly accepted the notion that a human being could be monetized and sold for profit. It took a civil war, presidential intervention, and congressional legislation to abolish this practice. In the first half of the 1900s, much of the marketplace encouraged racial discrimination in restaurants, retail stores, and transportation centers—to name but a few—which finally underwent correction as a result of civil rights protests, Supreme Court decisions, and congressional legislation.

When market entities fail to self-correct egregious moral and economic practices, the government eventually steps in to direct and compel change.[10] In addition to Sarbanes-Oxley, another prominent example of this in recent memory is a piece of legislation that the US Congress passed and became law. The bill is known as Dodd-Frank, named after its sponsors, Senator Christopher J. Dodd and Representative Barney Frank. The Dodd-Frank Wall Street Reform and Consumer Protection Act was passed in 2010 and signed into law by then President Barack Obama. It established "new government agencies tasked with overseeing the various components of the act and, by extension, various aspects of the financial system." The sectors of the financial system that now receive greater governmental scrutiny include "banks, mortgage lenders, and credit rating agencies."[11]

Both laws were enacted because companies and other financial institutions were not taking the needed steps to ensure that investors' capital was protected. So the US government responded to compel accountability and transparency. Sarbanes-Oxley, for example, seeks to protect investors in for-profit companies, and it has done this in many ways. According to Kayla Gillan, former deputy chief of staff to Securities and Exchange Commission Chairman Mary Schapiro, Sarbanes-Oxley has led to a number of beneficial results, including:

> public company internal controls are now much more ef-fective; independent auditors comply with stronger stan-dards and also have an independent regulator to oversee their efforts on behalf of investors and other stakeholders; audit committees must now be more competent and en-gaged in overseeing the audit and financial reporting; and the Securities and Exchange Commission must now spend more of its resources in reviewing the quality of informa-tion that companies provide to the market. . . . In short, [the Sarbannes-Oxley Act] has accomplished what it was designed to do—enhance investor protection.[12]

But do Sarbanes-Oxley and Dodd-Frank go far enough in offering the protections investors and stakeholders need? No, they do not. Federal legislation has overlooked an even more fundamental element in for-profits and nonprofits when it comes to the matter of protecting investors, donors, and stakeholders. This more critical element is the board-executive model that organizations use.

Today's organizational models actually make it easier for investors and donors to see their investments squandered. Investments can be lost through neglect, competitions for power among organizational leaders, conflicts of interest, and a host of other organizational problems that Sarbanes-Oxley and Dodd-Frank do not touch. In fact, the financial misconduct Sarbanes-Oxley was passed to address arose in the fertile soil of a board-governance model that still dominates corporate America and even some arenas in the nonprofit world. This model facilitated problems then, and it still does today.

Corporate America (and many nonprofits too) has a serious structural problem. Their boards are often so involved in operational matters that they fail to adequately carry out their responsibility to direct and protect the organizations they head. They are leading, managing, and even striving to accomplish the organization's work. As they do this, they are not ensuring that the best people and policies are in place to take care of investors, stakeholders, retirement plans, pensions, human-resource needs, information technology, and the list goes on. Sarbanes-Oxley and Dodd-Frank addressed the financial symptom of this structural problem, but the problem impacts so much else in an organization.

The best way to fulfill the letter and spirit of Sarbanes-Oxley (and its counterpart, Dodd-Frank) is through for-profits and nonprofits adopting a board-governance model that removes the top executive from a board position, clearly identifies unique and critical responsibilities and roles for the chief executive and board, and then unites and aligns the executive and the board in ways that are genuinely fruitful for their organization as well as for their investors and donors.

Aligned Influence—the board model I have developed and articulate here—is the new kind of governance model we need. It can and does truly protect investors and donors and their capital outlay, and it effectively accomplishes alignment throughout an organization. It fulfills and even advances beyond Sarbanes-Oxley.

Today's available board options have the same problem at their core: they fail to bring the board, the executive, the executive team, and the rest of the organization into the alignment needed to secure effectiveness, long-term sustainability and growth, and vital protections for investors, donors, and stakeholders. Aligned Influence is needed; otherwise misalignment and its attending consequences will continue to hamper and hurt for-profits and nonprofits, and those individuals invested in them, for countless years to come.

Organizational Health

Of course, organizations can be derailed in multiple ways. Competition from other companies, downturns in the nation's economy, a national or global economic crisis, resource scarcity, and natural disasters are just some of the *external* factors that can bring organizational havoc. To be sustainable, organizations need to have leaders and plans in place that can effectively take them through tough times brought on by such circumstances.

At the same time, organizations need to prepare for the more typical reasons for loss and failure—*internal* problems. Staff discontent and strife; competitions for power and control; divisions over organizational vision and purpose; disputes over hiring, budgets, and management decisions; customer complaints; job safety issues; and a host of other matters can undermine an organization and eventually topple it.

It's usually not one issue, external or internal, that leads to an organization's demise but the piling up of issues joined with the internal inability to lead through them and resolve them.

Organizations that are well ordered and well led within are best situated to persevere through the external crises that are beyond their ability to control.

The level of effectiveness needed to sustain organizations starts with and is maintained by the right organizational structure. Without that, even talented, creative, smart, dynamic individuals can become ineffective and driven away, thereby exacerbating their organization's crisis and becoming some of its fallout. Or such strong leaders can move on to other organizations, retire, or even be lost due to illness, accident, or death. When they are gone, organizations heavily dependent on them can easily fail and even come to an end.

It's true that success in an organization does not always mean that all is well. If your organization is doing well right now, ask yourself, *Are we doing well because of our good organizational structure or because of our situation?* If your organization's current state of health is situational—that is, you have the right executive director, good staff, market conditions are working for you, and so on—then I would urge you to use this moment to invest in your organization and make it structurally healthy. The best health is structural health; it's the most sustaining, enduring place to be.

Organizations suffer from internal conflict for a good reason: most of them attempt to operate day after day with boards, executives, and staff who are working with diverse and often divisive answers to questions that should reveal common understandings about organizational structure, authority, goals, objectives, commitments, values, and a number of other matters critical to an organization's identity, integrity, health, and success.

My reflections on the issues these questions and others like them raise and the answers they elicit have led me to develop an approach to organizational leadership and structure that takes seriously what other approaches tend to ignore, misunderstand, undervalue, or fail to adequately address, even if they admit their importance. My approach, Aligned Influence:

- Brings needed alignment throughout an organization
- Understands executive leadership and board oversight as unique influences
- Details clearly defined roles and responsibilities
- Takes the entire organization into account
- Helps organizations accurately identify whom they serve and whom they should protect
- Provides the proper structure for organizational sustainability and long-term effectiveness
- Clarifies why boards are mandated by the government

The most critical key to organizational health and success begins with an organization's structure, especially with its board of directors and chief executive officer. And yet, the approaches used today to address this structural issue are largely ineffective, even often harmful. In other words, zeroing in on the board and how it governs—to the near exclusion of executive directors—creates more problems than it solves. Moreover, putting all of one's attention on the executive director while virtually ignoring the board fares no better. On the other hand, bringing both the board and the executive director into the picture and striving to figure out how they can best relate to each other, while a better approach than the other two options, is also still inadequate.

Furthermore, none of the current models seem to understand, much less take seriously, what I have come to see is the most pressing and missing element in today's proposals: it's what I call the *ecosystem of influence* in an organization. No matter how finely tuned a board and chief executive are, if they fail to understand the organization they are trying to lead and the many other influencers in it, the organization will still flounder and may even collapse. And even if the organization still manages to succeed, leaders will never know for sure if their success was due to circumstances (e.g., key staff, market conditions, or a few budget items) or organizational structure. All organizations need an alignment of influencers that clearly defines roles and responsibilities from the top down, that helps ensure organizational integrity and sustainability, and that shows how to eliminate divisive competitions for power and control. Aligned Influence does all of this and more for organizations.

I have written this book so you and your organization can learn what Aligned Influence is, why and how it works, and what it can do to help your organization become healthy and successful internally and externally. I want to share with you what I have learned and proven effective—namely, that Aligned Influence presents a better way to structure and direct boards; empower executives; align all of the influencers in an organization; protect investors, donors, and stakeholders; and secure sustainability. Consequently, Part II of this book explains, illustrates, and supports the Aligned Influence model, while Part III talks about how to achieve alignment in an organization.

But before I introduce you to the Aligned Influence paradigm, I want to show you why it is needed. After all, proposals for boards, executives, organizational structure, and the like abound. "Answers" are plentiful. So why consider yet another proposal, a new approach?

My response is straightforward: because the other proposed "answers" are deficient in ways that matter. It's not just that they fail in some minor ways but that they fail in fundamental ways. What they miss or get wrong can actually harm your organization and its effectiveness. I have seen this repeatedly, and I have received reports from countless others "in the know" who have verified my conclusion.

In the next two chapters, then, I will take you through the major problems I have found with the answers typically provided. This will clear the way for explaining a much better approach to organizational health and success.

3

The Growing Discontent

As I travel around the country and listen to board members, executives, and other organizational leaders, I hear all kinds of complaints, criticisms, and struggles over whatever their current experience is with boards and executives and how they work together—or more accurately, how they don't seem to function well with each other. Many executives would like boards to have less authority and control or even be abolished. Many board members would like some of their executives to step away and move on or at least be less of a nuisance and more effective at what they have been hired to do. Such conflicts at the top have led many people to ask why boards are even needed in the first place. Can we dispense with boards?

Historically, boards came into existence many centuries ago and continued to be used for a number of reasons.[13] In reflecting on organizations that have boards today, I have concluded that no matter how widely organizations differ from one another, they all have at least one thing in common: *They manage someone else's money.* In for-profits that are publicly held, boards manage money coming from investors, and investors receive a return in dollars. If that financial return never comes or comes in at a significantly decreased level than expected, investors lose money and confidence in the company. Companies can experience investor backlash and even go out of business.

Nonprofits also receive money to manage. Their funds come from donors, which they then manage and invest in some value or service that donors expect to see fulfilled in communities of interest. If that value or service is not appropriately fulfilled, then donors have not received the proper return on their investment dollars. Nonprofits can then feel the sting of loss of donor confidence and future funds, which can upend these organizations, dwindle their size and potential effectiveness, and eventually lead them to close their doors.

Civic organizations, municipalities, and all the authorities they establish also receive funds in the form of taxes, and taxpayers expect their funds to be used wisely and for the good of the communities that these organizations have been set up to serve. When the public learns that their taxes have been misappropriated, squandered, or misused in other ways, their confidence in civic leaders wanes and they can seek out a variety of ways to speak up and take action. Civic leaders can experience job loss, court costs, public shaming, and other consequences as a result of financial mismanagement.

Because these types of organizations manage other people's money, they need oversight, and this is what a board is established to provide. In fact, the US government (as well as governments in numerous other countries) insists that boards be established for various kinds of organizations *because* boards are tasked to provide critical oversight for organizations that handle other people's money. Boards play other roles as well, but when they fail to protect investor and donor dollars, they create the kinds of problems that led to Sarbanes-Oxley and Dodd-Frank. When organizations fail to protect what and whom they ought to protect, the government will eventually step in and compel them to do what they should have done on their own.

Boards, then, are necessary. Acknowledging this, however, does not change the challenges within boards and between boards and executives. But it does highlight at least one critical reason for the existence of boards. And it should also suggest to executives why they should want a board—namely, to help them shoulder the privilege and responsibility of handling other people's money.

Granting, then, the need for boards, how should board members and executives work together?

Two Major Approaches to Governance

An organization with the complexity of having a board of directors and a chief executive officer have many models to draw on to help them decide how they can order themselves and their relationship for the betterment of their organization. Some of these models make the board the highest authority, others place the highest authority in the executive director, while still others divide authority between the board and the executive and strive to divvy up responsibilities between them in ways that will minimize confusion and maximize effectiveness so both can lead. No matter the model, they roughly fall into one of two approaches to governance: the traditional nonprofit model (the gears-apart approach) and the traditional for-profit model (the gears-overlapping approach).

Traditional Nonprofit Model: Extreme Separation

The most common governance paradigm is the traditional nonprofit one, which calls for an extreme separation between the board and the chief executive, as the next graphic illustrates:

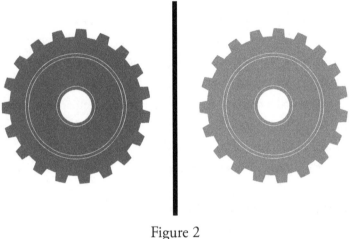

Figure 2

This approach is encapsulated in Policy Governance. Created by John Carver in the 1980s, this model assigns boards the job of generating policies that define the organization's "ends" or aims, how the board will govern the organization, and the limits the board will place on the executive director. As long as the chief executive remains within the board's established limits, he or she has broad freedom to determine the "means" needed to achieve the organization's board-approved ends.

On this approach, boards are encouraged against establishing committees; instead, board members are urged to work together as a whole on each matter under their purview. In other words, once the board has created various policy sets, which partly establish limits within which the executive director can perform his job, the board's role is then limited to ensuring that he stays within those assigned boundaries. Neither the board nor the executive director actually works with the other. The only real link between them is in the form of policies.

When I first began consulting with organizations, I drew on the Policy Governance model, which places a heavy emphasis on boards of directors. When boards are functioning well, organizations will too. At least that is the Carverite claim. But even an increasing number of Carverites are finding that the model they vouch for is not living up to its promise. There is a growing sense of discontent with Policy Governance among board members and executives. In some cases their organizations have spent tens of thousands of dollars to implement the model, expecting that they had finally found the answer to streamline the leadership of their organization and increase the organization's capacity to serve and produce.

But when the model failed to bring about these results, organizations were left disappointed, confused, and unsure where to look next for answers. In fact, I have talked to many organizational leaders who have concluded that the failure lies with them, not with the model. They think that if only they had worked harder or were more committed to their governing process, they would have been more successful. Other leaders have concluded that they simply were not smart enough to implement the model. They found it hard to understand, but rather than inferring that the model may be too complex, they decided that it must be good because it is so difficult to comprehend. The problem must lie with them, not with the model.

I understand this discontent with Policy Governance and models like it. I have been one of those leaders looking for answers. I understand the disappointment and confusion many have had with understanding these models, implementing them, and living with them. I understand the little voice inside that says, *I am a successful businessperson, community leader, entrepreneur, educator, etc.; governing an organization should not be as hard as these models make it.* And you are right. Governing should not be this hard; it should not be this complex.

Let's revisit the gears illustration for a moment. In Policy Governance and similar models, the board receives all of the attention, and it is directed to remain apart from the responsibilities and role of the chief executive. So between the gear of the board and the gear of the executive, a gulf of demarcation is set up. Neither gear can effectively touch the other one. Each gear turns at its own pace, existing in and of itself, doing its own work with little regard for the work of the other gear. Yes, the board lays down the policies that the executive must follow. And yes, the executive is expected to follow those policies and prepare reports that show his or her level of compliance. Beyond that, however, each gear functions on its own, focusing on its own limited sphere of influence (see Figure 2).

With the gears of the board and the executive separated like this, what guarantees that the gears will ever turn in a way where they get in sync? They never really link, so how can they ever match their movements in any productive way? And even if they do, what assurances are there that they will remain in sync?

There's little wonder why Policy Governance and similar models are falling out of favor with more and more organizations. These models are demonstrating their ineffectiveness to move organizations forward in healthy, successful ways. Instead, they provide increasing opportunities for boards and executives to operate independently of one another, to engage in turf battles, to hide issues from one another, and to create other dysfunctional problems that cost not just their effectiveness but that of the organizations they lead. And who gets hurt the most in the end? Investors, donors, and stakeholders.

Traditional For-Profit Model: Extreme Overlap

The other major approach to boards and executives working together can be pictured with two overlapping gears:

Figure 3

Notice here that the gears cannot work together any better than they do when they are separated. In fact, they get in the way of each other, which in some ways is worse than being completely separate.

It's common to find this model in publicly held companies and many civic governments that employ the "strong mayor" model. (It's also increasingly appearing in nonprofits, but more about that later.) I refer to it as the traditional for-profit model, and it typically manifests itself in the following way.

The executive director provides oversight of the organization along with accomplishing its operational matters. In effect, she does the board's work, even controlling what board members do. She may even reduce the board's role to that of an advisory committee, providing counsel but little else. The executive may deny that she is doing any of this, but the fact that she has a free hand and the board's hands are tied show otherwise.

Another way this approach could come out is through the board running the organization and its operations, even if board members claim they are not doing this. The board might accomplish this through establishing various committees (e.g., a committee on human resources, another one on finance, yet another on programs, still another on curriculum). These committees process information for the board and sometimes do some of the board's work. The board may even take a more hands-on approach, becoming entrenched in the day-to-day work of the organization. In this case, the board governs, manages, and even performs the organization's work. The executive director—assuming there is one—is largely a figurehead, there to do the board's bidding and nothing more.

No matter the manifestation, the extreme overlap of roles and responsibilities in the traditional for-profit approach displays misalignment as domination: either the board severely dominates the chief executive or the chief executive severely dominates the board. In both scenarios, misalignment reigns supreme.

This model also displays the duplication of functions. The skills, responsibilities, and roles of the executive are duplicated by members of the board. Whatever the executive can do, the board can do. Whatever the board can do, the executive can do. The board and the executive are mirror images of one another. The executive even sits on the board, usually as its chairperson, and board members are often paid to sit on the board.

This approach has not worked out well for the investors that a mandated board was created to protect. The Sarbanes-Oxley legislation was drafted to address financial problems that this governance model helped generate for investors. But it did not go far enough. Sarbanes-Oxley left the structural aspects of this board model alone, perhaps not seeing them as part of the problem or wondering if they were too entrenched in America's corporate mindset to command a change.

As common as this model is in the corporate world, discontent around it is growing. As Brock Romanek, editor of TheCorporateCounsel.net, commented, "the overhaul of corporate governance continues to be in its infancy as board failures remain too common, most institutional investors scarcely devote any resources to fulfilling their oversight roles, and too many managers fail to set a proper 'tone at the top.' "[14]

Common Reasons for Discontent

Other governance models exist beyond these, and while it can be helpful to explain and work through the strengths and weaknesses of every available board model, it can also be tedious and overwhelming. Rather than take that time, I can safely say that no board model to date has won the loyalty of all its users. In fact, there is a growing discontent among the users of all of today's board models. Fewer than ever are satisfied that their governance approach is the best one for their organization, whether it is a for-profit or a nonprofit.

No matter what model of organizational governance you use and the level of your discontent, I want you to know I have been where you are. I have been an executive and a board member. I have served under governance models that failed to help organizations in all the ways they were intended to.

As an executive, I understand that executives want to lead their organizations to new levels of success. They want to produce more, serve more, and provide more value with each progressing year of their tenure. They want to please their board and document their worth as a leader and manager, accomplishing all of this according to the direction and boundaries the board has established. However, sometimes executives feel like they do not have the sphere of control that they need in order to accomplish all that they desire. Sometimes they feel like they have to choose between serving their board and serving their clients. In some organizations this problem manifests itself as a board that has a strong set of governing policies but needs a great deal of support from their executive to do their work. In other organizations, the board has extended the reach of their governing activities into areas that the executive thought was his to lead. Now there is confusion about who is leading the organization—the board or the executive.

As a board member, I understand that board members really want to govern well. They want their board to be seen as mature, and they want to be seen as mature board members. They have sat through hours of board-policy-governance training sessions, and they are clear that they should "stay out of" the executive's work. They have worked hard on their board-governance policies and have been told by consultants that they generated a solid set of policies.

But now the question creeps in, *What do we now do as board members?* That little voice says that they should be doing something, surely something more meaningful, more vital than what many models dictate. They understand clearly what they should *not* be doing. What's not so clear is what they should be doing. They strongly sense that they are seen as leaders of the organization, but they don't feel much like leaders. Again there is confusion about who is leading the organization: Does the executive or the board lead it? This is a question of fundamental importance, and it strikes at the heart of the growing discontent over the available governance options.

According to many models, there is a difference between governing an organization and operating one. The board should govern it; the executive should operate it. That sounds simple enough. But is it an adequate answer? More and more organizations are finding that it is not. Something is missing, and the missing element is crucial to an organization's health and success. But before I focus on that, I want to delineate several problems I find with the common approaches to organizational leadership and structure. These observations are not just my own; they also come directly from the experiences of many others who work in this field daily.[15]

I use the term *governance models* to refer to all of the models that provide ways to structure organizations and their leadership. While the many contemporary models have significant differences between them, their similarities, especially in what they ignore or fail to deal with in an adequate way, are the main focus here. At the same time, I am not claiming that all of the current options lack value; one can find much good in several of them. I have retained the nuggets of insight and application other models provide, while incorporating those goods into a much better structure that truly fulfills their potential. The models in which they now exist do not serve them well. In Aligned Influence, however, they find a home more suited for them.

Problems with Today's Options

A Misplaced Emphasis

Every organization needs a set of governing policies. For example, in the Policy Governance model, there are governance process policies, ends policies, board-management delegation policies, and executive limitations policies.[16] Boards develop and use this policy set in order to give themselves and the organization direction and boundaries. These documents also provide legal parameters within which the board and its organization should operate.

Every organization should have a set of governing policies. But too many governance models overemphasize the role these policies should play. They give these documents a central focus rather than viewing them as important tools.

Governing policy documents are tools to support what boards do and don't do and why. A strong governing policy set also provides a board with the tools necessary to define the ends and limit the means of the organization. It gives the board the tangible means of speaking into the organization without getting involved in its day-to-day operations.

On the other hand, when governance models see these documents as more than tools, they help give rise to the very frustration that many organizational leaders experience. Boards end up working hard and spending a good deal of money to create these policy documents. With such a policy set done, boards then look for their work and money spent to begin to pay big dividends to the health and success of the organization. What they soon discover, however, is that these documents are incapable of bringing about any real change in the organization or accomplishing its work. Policies are tools but not problem-solvers. They can help us document solutions, but they are not solutions themselves.

I worked with one organization that had a Policy Governance structure solidly in place. The board had drawn on a Carver-governance consultant to bring them under the parameters of Policy Governance. They had followed this model for many years.

And because the organization was stable, the board concluded that everything was working well together. But when the organization faced hardships that severely upset its stability, the board began to feel as if they were not doing all they should to keep the organization afloat.

This led them away from their hands-off role under Policy Governance into taking on roles and responsibilities that their policies deemed inappropriate, at best. Their reliance on policies had failed to achieve the alignment needed between the board and the organization's executive director. And the policies, which the executive had relied on to keep the board out of his way, were inadequate to keep the board disciplined to their role. When the board finally called me in, the organization was in crisis mode. Their successful executive director was preparing to leave. The misalignment between him and the board had taken its toll. The extreme separation approach in governance highlighted rather than solved the alignment problem between the executive and the board. And it revealed the inadequacy of policies to achieve alignment as well.

People, not policies, bring about change and achieve goals. People apply policies, and people do not always see eye to eye on how policies should be implemented. In fact, the social structure at the top of organizations is a breeding ground for competition and conflict. Too often boards and executives end up pitted against each other rather than working together for the organization's development and success. A set of policy documents cannot adequately address these realities. A deeper and more comprehensive understanding of organizations, people, and groups and how they really work are needed.

Limiting Concepts

Ends and *means* are the key concepts of Policy Governance and similar models. Boards under these models know that they are to define the ends of the organization (its goals) and limit its means (how the goals are to be achieved). These boards know that, beyond these concepts, their golden rule is to stay out of everything else related to the work of the organization.

Now, the concepts of ends and means are helpful; they represent a very tangible way for a board to understand its role. However, when these terms become all-defining, they become all-confining. They so restrict the board that they lead many board members to become disconnected from the work of the organization and cause them to lose interest or personal investment in the organization.

This is ironic. When John Carver published his book *Boards That Make a Difference*, he wrote about some of the "cynicism and resignation" he had found among boards and chief executives. Rather than board members seeing dreams accomplished, visions achieved, and values implemented, they too often dealt with "trivial items," spent their time "reading reams of documents," participated in meetings that ran for hours and accomplished little, rubber-stamped staff recommendations, and took part in other activities that undermined or strayed far from the reasons that led them to serve on a board in the first place.[17]

Carver's model was developed to overcome such problems, to give board members more of what they had originally come to do. What his model actually too often produced, however, was greater disinterest among board members and a growing distance from their sense of involvement and engagement in the heart and soul of the organization they served. Under Carver, with board policies firmly in place, boards typically meet to listen to and read reports, vote on whether to accept the reports, and engage in other related activities that quickly become repetitive and lose their significance. Boards are told not to look behind the curtain that separates them from the executive and his team. Soon, board members conclude that they have little to do that actually helps their organization move forward. They have become disengaged from the organization's mission. They have no meaningful "to-do" role. In essence, what Carver meant to solve still persists as a problem.

We need to look for concepts beyond ends and means. We need a conceptual framework that encompasses far more, that delves more deeply into how organizations and boards actually function and points them toward how they can better function together.

Limited Focus on the Board

Models that put the board front and center naturally focus on developing the board and its members. For example, books that advocate and seek to implement Policy Governance even show this in their titles. Here's just a sampling: *On Board Leadership, Corporate Boards That Create Value, The Board Member's Playbook, Boards That Make a Difference, Reinventing Your Board, Making Diversity Meaningful in the Boardroom,* and *Getting Started with Policy Governance: Bringing Purpose, Integrity, and Efficiency to Your Board.*

Of course, boards matter. What they do, how they should be established, how they can run better, who should serve on them, and a host of other matters should be addressed and with beneficial results. Boards need development work. But once that work is done, many boards end up wondering why their huge investment of time and resources has not produced a commensurate improvement in the entire organization. The return they see on their investment disappoints them.

Such disappointing and frustrating outcomes point to a key flaw in these governance models. The flaw is this: they only develop one portion of those who have influence at the top of every complex organization. You see, in actuality, the board is not the only center of influence in the organization. There are other influencers. Improving just one influencer, the board, will not trickle down improvements to the other influencers, much less to the rest of the organization. Much more needs to be done.

A better approach to the health and success of an organization will take in the full reality of who has influence and power and how they can be developed and aligned in such a way that the entire organization benefits. This requires the development of both the board and the executive director. Focusing on just the board is inadequate. Whatever organizational model one uses, it needs to have, at the very least, everyone at the top of the organization in mind when considering its span of engagement. Any model—to be truly effective and beneficial throughout the organization and beyond—will have to speak to both the board and the executive, defining roles and responsibilities that complement the other.

I can hear some people arguing with me, saying, "But our executive goes to leadership seminars every year, so we on the board need further training too." While that may be true, let's consider what actually happens as a result. At those seminars, the executive is further equipped and inspired to "lead" the organization to new levels of success. Unfortunately, the board has heard similar messages from the consultants with which they work. Now both the executive and the board members are inspired to make a huge difference in the future of their organization on behalf of the community they serve. The problem is that they return to their organization only to find that they are once again tripping over each other as they both seek to do what they have been inspired to do. Conflicts remain; they may even be exacerbated.

What's the solution? The board *and* the chief executive need to be developed into an organizational team. Both need to understand and develop in their ability to execute their roles *together*. The board needs to understand their role and how it relates to the role of the executive and vice versa. The executive needs to understand that he has the ability and the responsibility to influence the future of the organization and that he serves as a part of a larger leadership whole—a whole that includes the board. Anything less than this approach condemns these influencers to the experience of constantly stumbling over each other, spending time and resources on negotiating their relationship rather than serving their clients.

Limited View of Roles and Responsibilities

For many governance models, their view of roles and responsibilities is too limited. Many of them define roles for the board only, speaking little to executive directors. Other models say much about executive directors but say little about what boards should do. And even those roles that are defined for boards or executives are typically inadequate, incomplete, poorly defined, and even conflicting. What we need are clearly defined roles and their ensuing responsibilities for both the board and the executive, and these roles and responsibilities need to be unique to each position, complementary to both positions, and active. Here's what I have in mind.

The roles of board members and executives need to be *unique*. In other words, board members need to have roles that do not conflict with but complement the executive's, and the executive needs to have roles that do not conflict with but complement those of the board. Clarity breeds confidence and engagement. Everyone in an organization benefits from being clear about what is expected of them, but it is particularly true for board members and executives. Roles that can be clearly articulated limit the amount of time that boards and executives have to spend trying to understand what they should be doing and how that relates to what others should be doing. In most organizations, boards and executives spend a great deal of time "negotiating" the allocation of power. This can be avoided if their unique roles can be defined. With this done, time can be recovered for building capacity and impact in the organization.

The roles of board members and executives also need to be *complementary*; in other words, their unique roles need to fit together well. Their different roles should run parallel, and when seen adjacent to one another, their mutually beneficial relationships should be easily recognized. When the board and the executive are fully engaged in their roles, they can do so without risk of interfering with the work of the other. They can spend their precious time and resources on the work of the organization rather than negotiating the line of demarcation between their roles.

Finally, their unique and complementary roles need to be *active*, giving both the board and the executive something worthwhile and beneficial to do. In the Policy Governance model, for instance, the board is repeatedly told to stay out of everything that does not relate to defining the ends or limiting the means of the organization. As a result, boards and their members become frozen and inactive in the organization's work.

Worse yet, the Policy Governance model and those individuals and groups who help boards implement it praise these hand-tied board members for staying out of the way of the organization's work. This leaves board members wondering, *What am I supposed to do now?* And the answer they too often find is that they end up doing little that they find productive and meaningful. And then there is the frustrated and often over-worked executive who wants his board's help in moving the organization forward, but he does not get that help from his board.

Limited External Relationships

Appropriate relationships with members of the organization's community of interest are critical to the organization and its work. On this, some governance models speak only to the board and instruct them to identify the "owners" of the organization—the ones for whom they govern. Other models give this responsibility to the executive director or they advocate for a team approach.

I think that a board should identify the community to which they are responsible. This will help board members determine the appropriate direction for their organization. But should such external relationships be the board's exclusive responsibility, as some models demand? No, not at all. This restriction actually ends up limiting the impact of the owners' community on the organization's work. It can also generate unnecessary and unbeneficial competition within the top of the organization.

An affordable-housing nonprofit's board chair and its executive director discovered this limitation in the Policy Governance model when they both included a certain city official in their planning discussions. The board chair and executive director found themselves competing for who should be managing this external relationship. It was not until they challenged their perspective of organizational roles and responsibilities that they discovered that both of them could have a relationship with that city official as long as their role and set of responsibilities were unique. They saw that to limit such relationships actually decreased the impact of both the board and the executive and what their organization could achieve.

A better approach would be one that recognizes that both the board and the executive are responsible for external relationships. The board should utilize external relationships to help them execute their unique roles and responsibilities just as should the executive. But their approach to these relationships should be based on their unique roles within the organization.

Limited Influence

Some governance models only address the influence of the board. The executive's influence is dealt with tangentially, only as it concerns the operation of the organization. This approach to influence leads to the perception that influence belongs to the board alone. Other models assert that the executive director has virtually all the influence, with the board having little to no say in what happens in the organization.

Both approaches are counterintuitive. Every person at the top of an organization appropriately believes that he or she has the commission and the ability to influence the direction and the work of the organization. And if this reality goes unrecognized, it inevitably leads to a battle over influence.

A better approach is one that acknowledges the existence of an ecosystem of influence that runs from the top to the bottom of every organization. Both boards and executives have the power to influence the organization's future as do other influencers in the organization. A new model should explain what these influences are, including how they are unique and should be complementary. The influence of one should not detract from the influence of the other. In fact, the influence of one needs to complement or support the other's influence.

Limited to Structures

For many governance models, the emphasis is on setting up structures, especially for the board. For example, certain models promote robust policy structures and define a role for the board that is primarily carried out around the boardroom table. These models tell the board to limit its activities to these things and leave the work of the organization to the executive and those under him. This approach provides little to no further exploration of human behaviors beyond these structures. And it certainly fails to address the relationship between the board and the executive, except to severely restrict it to compliance to existing laws and board policies. Consequently, it can only provide answers to issues that can be found within the structures themselves. Beyond that, this approach has little to nothing to contribute.

A better approach would take into account the presence and power of influence throughout the organization and would take seriously the fact that how influence is shared and channeled is just as important as the structures provided. In this approach, structures are tools designed to reinforce the roles and responsibilities that help to define and align the influences of all those people at the top of every organization. Both the board and the executive need to know that they can and should exert influence and that they can do so without competing for power with the other. Influence and power can be shared appropriately. Neither the board nor the chief executive should be placed in the position of cautiously walking an invisible line of demarcation between their roles, always fearing that something they are doing is impeding the other's ability to succeed.

Prescriptive Rather Than Descriptive

It's common for governance models to be *prescriptive*—to prescribe how the board ought to be arranged and function or dictate what the chief executive should and should not do. A prescription is an imperative; it says what should be. Do this. Don't do that. You ought to look and behave like this rather than like that.

Prescriptions are not bad, and they are found in all cultures and organizations. Governments lay down prescriptions in the form of laws. Moral codes are prescriptive, offering moral principles and commands to live by. Religions present shoulds and should-nots to their followers. Parents bring up their children with a host of commands and advice about how to think and live. Businesses too lay out parameters for conduct, including what violations can lead to discipline, correction, and even termination. Prescriptions help order our lives.

But where the prescription side of all the contemporary governance models has gone wrong is in their inability to see an entire organization as it actually is and actually functions. In other words, they have failed to be *descriptive* first. When we describe a fellow worker to someone, if we are to be accurate and fair in our description, we talk about the fellow worker's job skills, character, fit for the job, fit in the organization, interpersonal skills, and so on. The fuller the description we can give, the more accurate our rendering. But today's governance models do not do this when it comes to organizations. They do not seek first to see an organization as it is. Nor do they seek to understand what its employees, executive, and board are actually like and how they really work together. Instead, they begin and end with an organization's board or executive, telling that board or executive how they ought to function without first seeking any significant comprehension of the organizational context in which the board and executive function. This is a setup for failure.

Imagine that you have a computer problem. Something is not working correctly on your computer system, but you are not sure what the problem is. So you contact a computer expert to come check out your system to find the problem and fix it. The expert walks into your office, and without examining your computer first, sits down and tells you how computers ought to function. He gives you a schematic of a "typical" computer, discusses hardware and software—that may or may not be a part of your particular computer—and then tells you what you should do to ensure that your computer will work well. In the process you learn a good deal about computers in general and how they are supposed to work. Do you think, though, that you will learn what you need to in order to fix your specific computer? Are you getting the help that you really need to solve your particular problem? Sometimes you will, but mostly you will not. A theoretical and general understanding of computers can sometimes help us solve problems we have with our own computers, but we usually need more specific help and expertise.

This is a critical problem with today's governance models. And this omission is huge. Organizations have their own sociology, their own ecosystem, and every organization is staffed by people with their own character, worldview, agendas, skill sets, relationships, and understanding of the organization and their role in it. Such crucial factors make it clear that no two organizations are exactly alike. Whatever approach we take, then, when it comes to addressing organizational arrangements and relationships, must take into account what is actually common among disparate organizations and what is not. Coming in and dictating how a board, for instance, must be without first understanding the fuller organizational context in which board members are to do their work can easily lead to growing dysfunctions, disagreements, disappointments, losses, and ultimate failure.

The cure for this is understanding the ecosystem of influence. Before we delve into that, though, I want to address the most damaging effect of all of today's models—namely, the destructive competition for influence.

4

A Competition for Influence

Apart from Aligned Influence, the other governance models used today, even when applied well, generate a competition for power. Who leads the organization? How is this leadership to be carried out? Because the ecosystem of influence is ignored, the answers to these questions of leadership are inadequate and poorly informed. So board members and executives, all of who desire to see their organization succeed, end up running into and over each other. Arguments ensue over finances, new hires, process improvements, infrastructure, markets, effective marketing, and a host of other matters. Who has the authority to deal with what? Who steps in when responsibilities get dropped or mishandled? Who has the final word? In short, who guides the organizational ship and is responsible for keeping it afloat and moving it toward its prescribed destination?

According to some governance models, the board prescribes the ends of the organization. That is, the board designates in broad brushstrokes the intended impact of the organization, the group in or for which the impact is intended to occur, and the worth or priority of that impact. For example, a school board may designate that the K–12 school it governs will with equity accept and diligently instruct all students who enroll, and the school will perform this function for the purpose of furthering and securing the students' education and preparation for civil and vocational life in their local community and beyond. The school board may establish other complementary ends as well.

How will such ends be carried out, and who is supposed to be responsible for those ends being met? According to these models, the organization's top executive is responsible for this. She has the authority to define and establish the means for achieving the board's specified ends. The board can place some limits on the means, such as stipulating that the school's principal must oversee the school's hiring, manage its finances, and provide for its teachers' professional development in accord with local, state, and federal laws. But once the board designates the organization's ends and places certain limits on the means, the board's role reduces to governing itself and judging organizational—and thereby executive—performance. Are the ends being properly pursued? Are the means that the executive has set for the achievement of those ends accomplishing the intended task? Is the executive within reasonable parameters regarding her interpretation of the ends and limits that the board has established? These are the kinds of questions for which the board will seek answers.

This setup seems clear enough. The flow of authority is from the top down. The board is ultimately responsible for the entire organization, and the chief executive is there to carry out the will of the board. The executive is supposed to be free to hire who she needs to help her accomplish the ends laid out for her. The board oversees the executive, and she oversees everyone else. Clean and simple. Right?

No, it is not. This hierarchical arrangement of authority fails to take into account all of an organization's influencers and the directions in which influence flows. Influence doesn't just flow from top to bottom. It flows from bottom to top, from comparable positions to comparable and incomparable positions, from vendors to customers and vice versa. Influence is multi-directional, and influencers are found throughout an organization, not just in the boardroom and executive office. Who is supposed to direct all of this? Who has the responsibility of managing it? How are these influences supposed to be channeled?

The failure to address such questions leads to detrimental power plays occurring up and down an organization, including between the board and the chief executive. In fact, when boards and executives fail to understand or acknowledge how they influence one another and their organization differently, they destine themselves to implicitly or explicitly compete for the leadership of that organization. This competition for influence helps no one.

As I pointed out earlier, competitions for power are also found in other board models, such as those most often found in corporate boardrooms where the chief executive sits on the board as one of its members or even as its chair. This enmeshed form of leadership breeds internal competition and related problems, such as mistrust, hidden agendas, and self-protection.

Regardless of the governance model offered today, the most serious problem each one faces is the competition for influence and its numerous damaging effects.

The Competition's Effects

Competition's effects are multiple and varied. What follows is not an exhaustive list, but it includes the ones most prevalent in organizations today.

Effect 1: Portrays Influence as Limited and Mutually Exclusive

Most of today's governance models limit influence to the board and the executive. The board may prescribe the ends of the organization but not its means. The executive may control the means but only within the limits set by the board. So the board has influence that the executive does not, and the executive exercises influence that the board does not. Their separate spheres of influence are mutually exclusive—that is, the board's influence is not supposed to spill over into the executive's sphere of influence, and the executive's sphere of influence is not supposed to impact the board's sphere of influence.

Each party's influence is separate from the other; they exclude each other. As such, they are limited as well. The board is limited to the organization's ends, and the executive is limited to the organization's means. The executive should not seek to influence the ends, and the board should not work to influence the means.

But how does this arrangement work out in practice? Not well. In reality, influence cannot be contained so easily and cleanly.

Currently I am consulting with a board that has implemented the Carver model as fully as I have ever seen. The board has worked closely and consistently with a specialist in Policy Governance, and even he has said that the board is faithfully and fully carrying out the model. So have the separate spheres of influence remained separate?

No. One board member is competing for more power within the board itself and for greater power over the organization's chief executive. The executive is defending herself against this board member, and the other board members are torn between who they should believe and support—their fellow board member or the chief executive. As a consequence, some board members have decided to leave the board, and the executive is contemplating quitting as well. This competition for influence is tearing up the board, its relationship to the chief executive, and her relationship to it. Plus, all the energy they are expending on each other is achieving nothing beneficial for the organization they serve. On the contrary, the wreckage caused at the top is having a negative impact elsewhere in the organization, and even the organization's customers are feeling some of the fallout.

The reality is, boards and executives influence one another, and they influence other members of their organization. A governance model that fails to account for this lays the groundwork for unnecessary and destructive power plays.

Effect 2: Misappropriates Time and Energy Needed to Support the Organization

Time and energy spent competing for influence are time and energy taken away from supporting and advancing an organization.

In the above example, the organization is suffering because of the battle at the top. The board member attempting to challenge and further curb the executive's power and authority has forced the board to turn its attention inward on itself and to one step removed from itself—the chief executive. The executive is channeling her time and energy into fending off the board member's assault. The top of the organization is in turmoil.

In the meantime, the organization's needs for management, financial oversight and support, direction, and the like are put on the backburner. And some employees who assist with essential functions are pulled off of their tasks in order to supply reports and other forms of information to the executive and the board so the members at the top can advance their fight with one another.

Of course, not all competition for influence is as obvious as this. Much occurs under the radar.

- A board member subtly uses her influence on the board to shift support to her to become the next board chairperson.

- An executive, wanting a more sympathetic board, seeks to quietly influence board candidacy and elections so he ends up with more supporters on the board.

- A small group of employees, frustrated with their executive director, contacts a board member to plant thoughts about the executive's alleged incompetency and deception so they can get him removed.

- An executive director sees an up-and-comer in her organization, a person who may be more qualified for her job than she is. So she falsifies reports and uses innuendo and other techniques to marginalize this person or even find adequate justification for firing him.

- A board member has struggled with the way his organization's executive director has handled the company's finances, so he finds ways to rationalize his ever-deepening involvement in the financial side until he is either directly overseeing or actually managing the finances himself.

These are just some of the many hundreds of ways the competition for influence covertly manifests itself in an organization.

Effect 3: Generates an Unhealthy Internal Focus at the Expense of the External

When influencers within an organization remain unsatisfied with the influence they wield, they turn on other influencers within the organization, seeking to reduce or remove their influence and transfer it to themselves. This can show itself in a wide variety of ways as small as a fight of personalities or over a particular position, and as large as a push for organizational realignment or a redefinition of organizational purpose.

In one organization, their executive director was about to walk out the door. As I listened to board members and the executive, I learned that while the organization had followed Carver's Policy Governance model for many years, board members had begun getting involved in facilities maintenance and other operational activities that had been reserved to the executive. The board's crossover meddling led more and more staff to come to them with issues rather than to the executive and his team. So who now was in charge of operations? The executive or the board? The board's actions generated confusion among the staff and conflict between the board and the executive. If the conflict had continued unresolved, the organization would have lost an excellent executive director, and this would have affected the organization's ability to serve its clients and stakeholders.

However the competition at the top expresses itself, it compels an unhealthy turn inward. The influencers in an organization focus their energies internally rather than outwardly. What is happening inside the organization takes center stage while what the organization is supposed to achieve externally, for its clients, receives short shrift. Clients go unserved, or at least not served as well as they should be or even had been. Consequently, the primary reason for the organization's existence is undermined.

Internal struggles frustrate and even block external success and critical objectives.

Effect 4: Damages Relationships between Influencers

Whom do you trust?

When influence is used to compete for position, power, or prestige in an organization, trust becomes a casualty. For relationships within organizations to flourish for the good of the whole, trust must be established, maintained, and honored. The more trust wanes, the weaker relationships become. And when trust is violated, relationships often suffer irreparable damage.

Influencers who are engaged in power plays with one another generate distrust toward each other. The more that distrust grows, the harder it is for these influencers to collaborate constructively on the issues facing their organization. They see each other's moves as acts taken against them rather than as moves made for the organization's benefit. They work harder to preserve their turf and to advance their own agendas than they do in seeking solutions for organizational problems. Collaborations between them are strained and can even become intolerable and impossible. In the process, relationships are lost, and the organization incurs damage, internally for sure and externally often.

Effect 5: Leads to Discontent among Influencers and Beyond

Fights for influence® create discontent.

"You have more power than I do and I don't like it."

"You have all the power and I have none."

"You are not going to take power from me!"

When trust is undermined, suspicion replaces it. And discontent, suspicion's cousin, comes along to further affect the fight.

Discontentment is one of the great killers of motivation within organizations. It breeds distraction and apathy, anger and frustration, envy and jealousy, depression and deception, and many other negative attitudes and behaviors.

Discontent also leads to a hunger to leave the job one is in. According to a number of recent workplace studies and surveys, "the majority of people, quitting or not, are currently unhappy in their corporate jobs," writes Alan Hall of *Forbes*. Hall refers to one study that found that "a full 74 percent of people would today consider finding a new job. The most recent *Mercer's* What's Working study says 32 percent are actively looking."

Why the discontent? According to a study conducted by Accenture, 31 percent of employees dislike their bosses, the same percentage feel a lack of empowerment in their positions, 35 percent dislike the internal politics in their workplace, and 43 percent cite a lack of recognition for work accomplished as their rationale. Among Generation X employees (those born between 1966 and 1976), their greatest reason for discontent on the job is a lack of trust in their company.[18]

Discontent can lead good employees to leave, which in turn makes it that much harder for organizations to accomplish their goals and serve their clients. Contented workers may not always be happy workers, as the old adage claims, but they are certainly more satisfied and cooperative, much more likely to work toward organizational goals rather than against them, and much more likely to stay.

When influencers grow in their discontent, their dissatisfaction spills over into their other work relationships. Those under their influence pick up their snide remarks, their criticisms, their apathy and distrust, and the many other ways they express their unhappiness and restlessness. The influencers' discontent grows among many of those over which they have sway. Soon it can affect whole departments and divisions, and sometimes it can even spread throughout the entire organization.

The more the discontent spreads, the more likely it is to start revealing itself to the organization's clients. They see and hear the poor attitudes and affected performance of those they connect with in the organization. The way they are served suffers, so their contentment with the organization begins to turn into a growing discontentment. And this may lead them to seek the fulfillment of their needs elsewhere, while at the same time urging other clients of that organization to make the same move.

When discontentment appears at the top of an organization, whether at the board or executive level, its impact can filter down the organizational ladder quickly if left inadequately addressed. Just as psychological depression can negatively affect one's body, so discontent at the head of an organization can detrimentally affect the body of employees it leads. While influence is multidirectional, its top-down flow is most important to the health and success of an organization. Problems at the top, including discontentment, must be solved for an organization to survive and thrive.

But discontentment at the top is a problem that many governance models actually help create. Though they do not cause this problem intentionally, their design actually serves to generate discontent among board members and executives. There must be a better way.

Effect 6: Destines a Less Effective Use of Donors' Funds

In an organization that depends in whole or in part on donations, power plays at the top frustrate the effective use of donor dollars. How should the monies be spent? Who is ultimately responsible for their distribution? What is the best use of the funds? Answers to these questions and others can display divisiveness rather than unity when competitions for influence are active and inflamed.

The competitors may herald the good of the organization, and some of them may actually have that in view, but the resultant feud brings little to no good to anyone, including the organization. The time they spend fighting each other steals time away from effectively addressing the problem they were established to solve. The energy that would typically go into determining how best to use the funds received is channeled into lesser matters that usually have more to do with ego than with the achievement of a common mission.

Effect 7: Makes the Organization Less Attractive to Donors and Grantors

Causes that develop around real or perceived needs for change do not create, earn, give, and spend money—people do. Behind every donation and grant are people. While they give their dollars to causes and institutions they believe in, they would not give those dollars if the people they handed the monies to were untrustworthy, unreliable, or lacked the ability to accomplish what they said they could. In other words, when all is said and done, people give to people—people they can count on to do what they believe needs to be done.

Suppose these givers discovered that their dollars were going to people who were not directing and managing their organization well. Suppose they found out that those at the top of the organization were squabbling among themselves over the organization's mission, leadership needs, financial expenditures, or other matters that had a significant impact on the organization's ability to accomplish its stated goals. How do you think those givers would regard that organization? Would they see it as a great place to put their money? Likely not.

The organization's attractiveness is affected by the tone, attitudes, character, and unity of those at the top. With regard to the competition for influence, the more obvious it becomes, the more it projects a harsh tone, poor attitudes, questionable character, and division—not the kinds of things that promote a desire to give and a conviction that the money will be used well.

Effect 8: May Fail to Attract Potential Board Members and Executives

Power plays at the top, especially within the boardroom and between board members and executives, make it difficult to attract new members to the board or new hires at the executive level. If such competitions for influence are also showing up at the division and department levels, it makes it additionally hard to find new talent for the top spots. Why enter a battle that isn't yours? Why accept leadership in an organization where you will be challenged, undermined, or petitioned to take sides as soon as you walk in the door? Leadership certainly comes with a cost, but is this particular cost worth the personal and professional price? Few would say yes and step into the fray. Fewer still would later agree that they had made a good choice.

I was contacted by a charter school that was interested in learning more about Aligned Influence. But the board continued to delay my time with them because they kept losing board members. So I finally asked them, "Which comes first—fixing your organization so you can attract and retain the right board members, or retaining the right board members so you can move toward fixing the organization?" Most often you have to make the investment to fix the way organizational influencers are aligned before you can attract and retain the right influencers—or, in this case, board members.

The same is true when it comes to executives. Repeatedly I have come across organizations that have lost one director after another because of the misalignment among influencers. Many times these organizations want to wait to have me come in until they hire their next executive director and get him or her established. But this is a mistake. Waiting to fix the alignment problem will not help an organization find the right person. Rather, fixing the alignment problem will enhance an organization's ability to find the right person to lead them.

Effect 9: Severely Restricts the Collaboration of the Board and Executive in Decision-Making

When board members and the executive are fighting over influence, they are not inclined to work well together toward solving an organization's problems. And when the board proposes solutions, the executive may not put her full energy behind implementing them. Or when the executive comes up with solutions, the board may not approve them. And when the board and executive are supposed to come together to generate problem-solving ideas, discuss their merits, and settle on which ones to implement, their mutual trust will be at a low ebb, so whatever they decide will not have the full engagement of either party.

Indeed, the issues faced by board members and executives in problem-solving will surface in virtually any significant decision-making they must engage. The organization's mission, customers, finances, structure, philosophy—anything that requires board members and executives to work together for a common goal—will be limited by the severity of the competition for influence among them. Organizations need their boards and executives unified and fully engaged. To the degree that deteriorates, organizations suffer loss.

The loss can be in such tangibles as personnel, profits, donations, grants, the number of customers served, and the number of products produced. The loss may also be in intangibles such as the organization's direction, the morale of its workers, the satisfaction of its customers, and the way it is perceived by the pool of potential new employees. When enough losses accumulate or the more critical ones occur, an organization's reputation and the reputation of those who lead it can suffer tremendous damage, and it will take much more than a slick and savvy publicity campaign to overcome that wreckage.

Effect 10: Uses Reinforcing Messages to Further Entrench an Unhealthy Resolve

I know a board that has been told by its Carverite specialist that it is running exactly as it should. Yet, some of the board members have come to me wringing their hands, feeling as if there is nothing more they can do to save the organization they oversee. After all, they have implemented Policy Governance fully and accurately. What else can they do?

The executive of this organization has his own resources for consultation. They have told him that he is doing all he needs to do for the organization he leads.

So the executive blames the board for the organization's failings, while the board blames him for those same failings. Each stands entrenched in their rightness, pointing fingers at the other for their wrongness. The blame game is typically another manifestation of the competition for influence. But notice that in this case, the blame is charged to each party's account by the reinforcing messages each has received from others.

Consultants, conferences, websites, books, journals, magazines . . . there are numerous resources available for boards and for executives. Boards find in these resources "tried-and-true" ways and creative new ways for leading their organization. Executives find similar counsel presented to them. Both parties are told how they can better lead their organization. So they respectively return to the boardroom and executive office inspired and ready to put the counsel into practice. But as they do, board members often find the executive resisting and challenging the board's new proposed approach, seeing it as an infringement on the executive's authority and power. And when the executive puts his new plans and procedures into place, board members complain, believing that he has usurped or trampled on their authority to lead.

Each party appeals to their respective authorities on the matter to justify their perspective and stance. Tempers rise. Arguments proliferate. Trenches are dug. More reinforcing authorities are consulted. The competition for power heightens. And the divide between board and executive widens into an unbridgeable gulf. If no compromise can be reached, if no peace treaty signed, if no better paradigm found, the organization will flounder and fail, and all will be out of a job.

The Way Forward

The competition for influence can be beaten back, but wherever there are human beings, it will never be eliminated. On the other hand, its frequency can be greatly reduced and its impact virtually nullified. But for this to happen, changes at the top of an organization must occur. The way top leaders establish, organize, direct, and execute their various roles and responsibilities must model what real cooperation and beneficial forms of influence actually look like. And those at the top must insist, encourage, and inspire such aligned influences throughout the rest of the organization they lead. This is the way forward.

The way forward is *not* through more effective ways to fight for power.

The way forward is also *not* through a better implementation of today's ultimately ineffective governance models.

Rather, the way forward involves boards and executives embracing their unique and critical roles and learning how they can work together in harmony to positively influence their organization and the community of interest it serves. The way forward involves understanding an organization's ecosystem of influence and aligning those influences for the good of the whole organization. This is the way of my new paradigm, Aligned Influence. And this will be the focus of the rest of this book.

PART II

Aligned Influence—The Way Forward

5

The Ecosystem of Influence

The way forward begins with understanding and working with the *ecosystem of influence.*

In the world of nature, an ecosystem is a complex set of relationships between the living things and the nonliving things in a given environment. The environment can be as small as a pond or tree or as large as a lake or forest. And the living things can be animals, microbes, and plants. A healthy ecosystem is one that usually displays biodiversity, balance, and order between the living and nonliving things in that environment. Each member carries out its function in ways that partake of the environment, sustain it, and enhance its survival and ability to thrive. The healthier the ecosystem, the greater ability it has to withstand and overcome even severe natural occurrences, such as storms, tornadoes, hurricanes, floods, fires, and earthquakes.

Organizations are much like ecosystems. Whether an organization is small or large, a start-up or firmly established, for-profit or not for-profit, religious or secular, it is a complex set of relationships between the living (employer, employees, board members, executives, customers, clients, and so on) and the nonliving (rules, procedures, policies, plans, furniture, buildings, and so on). And each living member within the organizational ecosystem has a role to play and responsibilities to carry out.

When members fulfill their functions well, they enhance the organization's ability to survive and thrive no matter what else occurs in the surrounding environment, such as economic downturns, greater government intrusion, and shifts in the marketplace. Even internal changes, such as board turnover or changes in executive or mid-management leadership, can be withstood and successfully overcome. All depends on how well an organization's ecosystem runs, which includes how it is maintained, supported, and directed.

None of today's governance models take the ecosystem of an organization into account either at all or in any significant way. Policy Governance, for example, focuses on board development. Other models emphasize the role of the executive to the near exclusion of the board. While still other models seriously consider the development of the executive and the board and their relationship, they still ignore the organization as a whole. The truth is, an organization's ecosystem is richer, more complex, more nuanced than any of the contemporary governance models recognize. The ecosystem has many more influencers than any of the models address.

Notice I said *influencers*, not leaders. *Leadership* is a loaded term that when used in discussions of organizations is usually restricted to board members, the executive director, and maybe other top-level executives. I prefer to use the term *influence* instead. At the heart of leadership is the ability and need to influence. In fact, leadership expert John C. Maxwell observes, "If you don't have influence, you will *never* be able to lead others." He goes on to say, "Titles don't have much value when it comes to leading. True leadership cannot be awarded, appointed, or assigned. It comes only from influence, and that cannot be mandated. It must be earned. The only thing a title can buy is a little time—either to increase your level of influence with others or to undermine it."[19]

Leadership, then, is influence. Leaders have followers. They know how to persuade others to listen to them, trust them, believe in them. A job title may shout, "Person in charge!" But the person holding that job title is only truly in charge when he or she can persuade people to participate.

When leadership is understood as influence, one can more readily see that influence happens throughout the ecosystem of an organization. Of course, board members and executives exercise influence, but so do division and department heads, managers, people in charge of overseeing contract labor . . . indeed, virtually anyone who holds sway over others in the work environment is an influencer. In educational institutions, influencers would include school board members, superintendents, principals, vice principals, department chairs, counselors, teachers, secretaries, and the like. Influencers in local churches would include ministers, elders, deacons, Sunday school teachers, music directors, small group organizers and leaders, and so on.

From the top down, influencers can be found doing their work and guiding and helping others in their work. And all these influencers exercise whatever persuasive power they have through a variety of means, including processes and policies, goals and objectives, and rules and procedures. The living members affect the interpretation, implementation, and sometimes even the viability of the nonliving members.

So the answer to the foundational and critical question "Who leads your organization?" is actually multifaceted and complex. On one level, your board and your top executive lead your organization, or at least try to. But under them are a host of other leaders who influence your organization as well. And at every level, the balance and viability of the ecosystem depends on each of its members to accomplish what they are assigned to do, and to do their work and carry out their influence in ways that align with the other members and their roles, responsibilities, and influence. A breakdown at any level, but especially at the top, will upset the organization's ecosystem and threaten its balance, its integrity, its viability, and perhaps even its existence. To achieve a well-functioning organization, its influencers must be identified and aligned.

When I think of the metaphor of an ecosystem as applied to organizations, eight terms come to mind that fill out this metaphor and show how applicable it is to human organizations. Let's consider each term.

Explaining the Ecosystem
Ordered

Ecosystems, whether in the world of nature or the human world, exhibit a sense of order. The order may not be immediately apparent, and it may not be all it can be or should be, but order is there nonetheless. Events occur, members act and react, dependence and independence are exemplified, roles are played out. When all that is there and all that occurs are taken into careful consideration, one can see that the ecosystem has an arrangement, an order, by which it works.

In organizations, we want this order to work for the benefit of the whole as well as for the parts. The skill set, roles, and responsibilities of each member, ideally at least, should be matched to an organizational need so the whole will function as it should and the member will recognize her value to the overall objectives and goals.

This applies to board members and executives too. Their place in the organization and how they carry out their roles and responsibilities are critical to the overall health and achievements of the organization they seek to influence and serve. Confusion, frustration, or competition for control and direction that occurs among these influencers can strain and even shatter an organization's order. The ecosystem will suffer losses that may never be retrieved, though they may be overcome if the proper work is done to restore the needed order.

Inevitable

All ecosystems, including human organizations, display order, and this is inevitable. We not only have a desire for order in our lives, but order occurs whether we consciously seek it or not. We seek to fit in, to find our place, to figure out how things work, to reorder what we find unsuitable or unworkable. We desire order. We search and work for it. And when we look at the natural world, we find order as well. Animals, plants, lakes, seas, oceans, wind, rain, snow, even tornadoes and earthquakes, all exhibit order, patterns, arrangements. Our ability to predict natural events and develop theories about the earth's past and present happenings are all built on our understanding of the way nature is ordered. And when we reach out into space with our telescopes and probes, we find an even greater intricate web of organization. Order is present, no matter where we look.

Disorder occurs as well. But there can be no disorder apart from order. Order is primary; it's foundational to the universe, our earth, and our organizations. Disorder is like a parasite or rust. It occurs unwelcomed, and its host—that upon which it lives and works—is order. We can live without disorder, but we cannot live without order.[20]

Likewise, organizations will strive for order and will seek to maintain it and even enhance it. This is their nature. An organization that seeks disorder is seeking its own demise. And wherever disorder reigns, organizations die.

So while some type of order is inevitable, the right type of order for any given organization is not. Order will occur, but it may not be the kind of order an organization needs for long-term survival and success. The various members of an organization will push and pull within their positions and beyond in search of an order they think they need. They will use their influence to try to achieve this desired order. Therefore it is critical for executives and boards to understand the ecosystem of influence within their organizations so they can best learn how to order their organizations and thereby properly harness and direct the many influencers.

Interdependent

Order is achieved, at least in part, through interdependence. We see this in nature's ecosystems with, for instance, plants depending on water, oxygen, and sunlight, and then the animals that eat the plants also depending on water and oxygen. Take away the water and the plants will eventually die. And with the death of the plants, the animals depending on them will move on, if they can. Remove the oxygen and neither the plants nor the animals will survive.

Likewise, in the human ecosystems called organizations, interdependence exists. The organization's success, even survival, depends on the board and executive fulfilling their roles and meeting their responsibilities. If they fail, the organization suffers, and it can even face such losses that it may not last. Moreover, if vice presidents, directors, or managers undermine the board or chief executive, the organization can also be damaged but it may not collapse. All depends on how well the board and executive deal with the damage and those who caused it.

For organizations to maintain right order, they need board members and executives to work and develop together. Leaders who go rogue, especially those in the boardroom or the executive office, can create havoc. The ecosystem of influence, from the top down, must recognize the interdependence of its members and their importance to the proper functioning of the whole organization, not just of its parts.

Complementary

Interdependence includes complementary relationships. These are relationships that fit together, that when properly aligned they uphold and strengthen one another. Each member of the relationship may not be equal in influence, authority, responsibility, or role, but each member matters to the relationship's maintenance and growth. Consequently, each member is important; her contribution is valuable and worthy of respect. The whole would not be what it is apart from the contributions of its members.

All of this applies when it comes to the matter of influence. While many members of an organization exercise influence, some have greater influence than others, and some have influence that runs horizontally (e.g., between fellow tech analysts) while others have influence that travels vertically (e.g., from a division leader to her managers, or from a manager to his division head). Still, the influence exercised needs to be complementary; it needs to fit within, not compete against, the organization's structure and mission.

Imagine a triangle of two-by-four boards. Two boards have been set up in an "L" shape, with the third board laying at an angle at the other boards' ends. Each board is dependent on the other to remain in a triangular shape. Their interdependence makes their triangular order possible, and their interdependence would not come about, much less last, unless the relationship between the boards was complementary. Furthermore, each board affects—influences—the ability of the other boards to stay in place.

Now, suppose these boards could think, feel, and choose, and one of them decided that it wanted to take the place of one of the other boards. This competition for place could result in the collapse of the triangle. But suppose that the other two boards used their influence to help the third board understand how critical its role was to the structure of the triangle, that without its cooperation and its appropriate use of its influence the triangle's integrity could be seriously compromised. Would the triangle's structure become more secure? Would the third board finally grasp how it fits with the others and find a source of satisfaction with that fit?

Now apply this illustration to your organization. Influencers abound in your organization. As long as they exercise their influence in ways that complement your organization's structural and missional integrity, your organization will likely remain intact and grow. But if one or more of these influencers use their power to achieve their own ends over and against that of your organization, especially if they manage to bring other influencers alongside them, your organization will suffer internal strife that can spill over into its ability to service its customers. The ecosystem will suffer. It may even be brought down.

How complementarity operates or fails to operate in your organization must be understood and effectively addressed if you are to do more than just limp along in your drive to survive and succeed.

Balanced

Order.

Interdependence.

Complementary relationships.

All of these require the proper balance. Shift the balance in a natural ecosystem—such as add too much water or let the water source dry up—and a beautifully arranged stream with a growing trout population may turn into a raging river or a dried-up riverbed that threatens the trout that depend on it. Balance matters.

Human organizations operate similarly. When organizations become top heavy, those below suffer and that affects the entire organization. When organizations lose needed leaders or cannot maintain enough talented workers to follow, the pain can also be felt throughout the organization.

The same happens when we consider power and influence within an organization. Influence is power wielded with a purpose, with an end in view. It is power channeled to reach an objective or a goal. Power itself can be withheld or exerted, and it can be used to help or hurt. The greater the power, the greater the influence, and the greater potential there is for producing order or disorder, success or failure, internal satisfaction over dissatisfaction, apathy, and strife.

So in an organization, influencers need to use their power for the benefit of the organization. This requires that the influencers at the top are aligned in their roles, responsibilities, talents, and even in their movements toward common goals, and that they are seen as worthwhile models for how the influencers below them use their power. When power and influence are balanced at the top, there's a better chance that they will become balanced throughout the organization. Of course, this does not occur by accident. Balance is achieved intentionally and wisely. And once achieved, it requires processes of maintenance for it to remain.

Able to Be Protected and Improved

Work in environmental science over the last century has taught us much about what human beings can do to help protect and improve existing ecosystems. Our growing knowledge and experiments in applying it have led to vast improvements in waste and water management, pollution control and cleanup, safety in drilling and shipping, and so much more. This work has required great determination and commitment, but it has paid great benefits for the natural and human orders.

When we turn our eyes toward our organizations, we can readily see that they too need protection and improvement. It's all too easy for organizations to tend toward disorder, for people and processes to work at cross-purposes, to become counterproductive. We need to protect what we have achieved and look for ways to further advance the entire organization and its effectiveness.

The same applies to boards and executives. They can become complacent, thinking they have arrived at a comfortable place so they can now coast the rest of the way to success. Or they can become overzealous, grasping for power and prestige that manages to undermine what has been achieved. One critical way an organization's board members and executive director can protect and improve their organization is by exercising the commitment and courage to play their distinctive roles well rather than trying to undermine or take the place of each other's role.

Susceptible to Sub-optimization

W. Edwards Deming was a renowned statistician and business innovator whose work in war-torn Japan after World War II played a decisive role in that country's economic recovery and resounding success. In 1982, Deming wrote a book titled *Out of the Crisis* that focused on American businesses and their needs. In that book he presented a theory of management that showed "how American companies require nothing less than a transformation of management style and of governmental relations with industry." Deming presented his principles of management transformation and showed how to apply them.[21]

In his work on managerial transformation, he noted that "a system is a collection of components that interact and have a common purpose and aim." Those who manage the components of a system "should promote the aim of the entire system," and this may require that they sub-optimize some of the system's components.[22] However, any and all sub-optimization of components must always take into consideration the affect it will have on the whole system. If sub-optimization will benefit the whole, then it should be done. If it won't do this, then it should not be done, even if it benefits one of the system's parts. In other words, while sub-optimization of the parts may optimize the whole, it does not always work that way.

To see this, consider a group of shepherds who share the same pasture. All the shepherds use this common pasture as grazing land for their sheep. One of the shepherds decides that he can increase his profits by adding one sheep to his herd, an addition he makes. The other shepherds see this, and each one decides that he can increase his profits by adding his own sheep to his herd, which each shepherd does. While the shepherds' actions have, in the short term, optimized each of their profits, the long-term effect becomes counterproductive to the system as well as to the parts.

Over time, the system of the shepherds deriving common benefit from sharing the same pasture starts to break down, for the additional sheep have reduced the grass available to the various herds sharing it. This, in turn, reduces the food intake of the sheep and therefore the sheep's quality and even quantity. Some sheep end up with inadequate amounts of food and therefore suffer and even die. So what began as sub-optimizing the profits of each shepherd has led to the overgrazing of the common pastureland and its eventual exhaustion, which has also negatively affected the profit that could be made from the sheep. Sub-optimization of a part—namely, attempting to increase the profit margin of each shepherd by adding new sheep—failed to optimize the whole and led to loss that affected the whole.[23]

Consider a business venture that focuses on reducing its production and delivery costs but, in the process, ends up reducing its revenues. Or a university that responds to the theft of some of its books by barring all students from its libraries, thereby seriously impinging on students' abilities to conduct needed research for school projects. Or a government agency that promotes a social program for its benefits but fails to take into serious consideration its costs, which in time significantly outweighs its benefits.[24] In each case, the sub-optimization of a system's parts has actually hampered the health and success of the whole.

The ecosystem of influence within an organization is a complex of interdependent relationships that, when properly supported and balanced, will positively impact the whole. Boards and executives do not function in isolation of the whole organization and neither do any other of the organization's parts. For an organization to grow and become healthy, the whole needs to be addressed, not just some of its parts. Sub-optimization produces sub-optimal results.

Policy Governance's focus on the board is sub-optimization at work. While the board may undergo some improvements, the organization likely will not. In fact, the organization may even suffer some losses because the focus has been too narrow; the organization's leaders have not understood, much less accounted for, the organization as a whole and the ecosystem of influence that drives it. Since boards and executives are ultimately responsible for the organization as a whole and not just for some of its parts, their failure of not giving the whole the attention it deserves and needs becomes a high-order failure with potentially damaging and wide-ranging consequences that may become irreparable.

Complex

If all of this sounds complex, it is—on one level. Ecosystems are dynamic, a web of relationships between various things and processes that are interdependent in some ways and independent in others. For instance, while numerous living things depend on the sun for light, the sun does not need life for it to exist or operate.

Likewise, human organizations are ever-changing webs of relationships between the personal and the interpersonal, the individual and the group, the employees and the customers, the executive director and the board, the mission and the methods, the profits and the expenses, company policies and state requirements, and hosts of other factors. How can all of this be understood so that an organization can be effectively established and aptly motivated to move forward in the ways that will accomplish its mission? Can the complexity of the ecosystem of influence be simplified so it can be developed for an organization's benefit?

The answer lies in the Aligned Influence model. Contrary to the other governance models, Aligned Influence begins and ends by considering organizations holistically. It understands and operates in light of the ecosystem of influence. This model grasps what the others do not and, within the strictures of their systems, cannot. By viewing the whole, the macro level, Aligned Influence makes it easier to define, understand, and enhance the whole, which benefits the parts. By focusing on organizational development, the best aspects of sub-optimization can be properly employed and the worst aspects avoided. The complex can be appropriately simplified in ways that build trust, enhance freedom, increase health, and provide holistic direction for ongoing development and growth.

Giving Influence Its Proper Due

So, the bottom line is this: among all of the problems plaguing the other governance models, the most serious and far-reaching one is their failure to deal with the ecosystem of influence resident in all organizations. When a governance approach singles out just one part of the ecosystem for development, it sub-optimizes this one part to the exclusion of the whole. This is the primary reason for the growing discontent over the other governance models. They cannot answer such essential questions as:

- How does the board influence the organization differently than the chief executive?
- How do those kinds of influences relate to one another?
- How are the roles of the board and the executive interdependent but unique?
- How should their roles fit with, harness, support, and direct the organization's other influencers?

- How can those other influencers (managers, employees, faculty, volunteers) best work with the leaders at the top (board members and executives) to advance the organization's success?

The answers to these questions start to give the role of influence its proper due. And as that becomes clear, it demonstrates that today's common governance models are not addressing the full scope of the nature and needs of the organizations they seek to help. We need a better, more holistic approach. We need what Aligned Influence provides.

6

The Aligned Union of Influence

The cure for competition within an organization is collaboration. When boards and executives collaborate internally rather than compete with one another, they can influence their organization in ways that will achieve the excellence and success they all want. An apt metaphor for this relationship is a yoke.

Yokes have been used in my family for several generations because many members of my family were farmers. My grandfather was one, and he often spoke of farming with horse-drawn equipment instead of tractors. Sam and Jeff were the names of the last horses he used; he named them after his grandfathers, Sampson Johnson and Jefferson Elliott. My grandfather liked Sam and Jeff and did a good deal of work with them. The key to his team's success was that Sam and Jeff, when yoked together, did not fight each other but pulled together evenly against the yoke. Their collaboration accomplished the work needed, making it a joy to work with them.

When boards and executives pull together rather than compete against one another, they too can better accomplish the work of the organization. As they both fully engage their respective roles of influence, together their efforts will significantly and effectively improve their organization and better serve those who benefit from the organization's work.

Aligned Influence shows how to accomplish this goal. This model focuses on both sides of the yoke—the board and the executive director. And it takes into serious consideration the rest of the ecosystem of influence, which includes other key influencers in the organization. Aligned Influence shows how the board and the executive can be yoked together to pull the organization evenly and therefore effectively and beneficially, creating a healthy and successful organization from the top down.

Aligned Influence: An Overview

The Aligned Influence model defines the role of both the board and the executive and how they influence the organization, stressing that the key to organizational success is aligning their respective influences appropriately—in other words, how they can collaborate rather than compete. It lays out the structure of this organizational unity via three ordered pairs of responsibilities, one set belonging to the board of directors and the other set to the executive director. Aligned Influence also shows which pairs of responsibilities are linked and how they should function together to pull the yoke of the organization.

- The board *directs* the organization, and the executive *leads* it.
- The board *protects* the organization, and the executive *manages* it.

- The board *enables* the work of the organization, and the executive *accomplishes* it.

The board's side of the yoke is to direct, protect, and enable the organization. The executive's side is to lead, manage, and accomplish the work of the organization. Stated another way, the board exercises its influence through directing, protecting, and enabling, while the executive funnels his influence through leading, managing, and accomplishing. Only by fully leaning into their portion of the yoke together will the board and the executive director ensure that the organization is successful. Aligning their influence for collaboration is the key.

Here is a clear and easy way to visualize these varied roles and responsibilities:

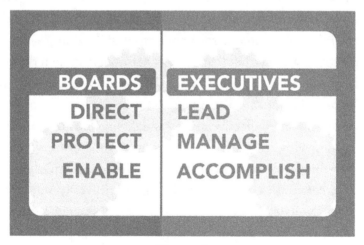

Figure 4

If we return to the gears illustration, here's what Aligned Influence achieves, not just at the top but also throughout the organization:

Figure 5

Notice that the top gears representing the board and the executive are securely joined. They don't overlap each other or sit separate from each other. They are aligned in a way that complements their unique roles and responsibilities and sets them up for cooperation rather than for competition. And then the gears under them, which represent the rest of the ecosystem of influence in the organization, are also linked with the top gears to promote cooperation and effectiveness throughout the organization. Everything works together for the common good of the whole.

For this level of alignment to be achieved, it must start at the top, between the board and the top executive. In subsequent chapters, I will delve into the roles of the board and chief executive and show how each unique pair aligns. Here I will provide a brief description of each role so you can begin to see what Aligned Influence is all about and how it can help your organization.

The Board of Directors' Role

Under Aligned Influence, the role of the board of directors is to direct, protect, and enable. Here is what I mean.

First, the board *directs* the organization by establishing and maintaining the strategic *what* of the organization. What should the organization do? What should the organization accomplish? Whom should the organization serve? What ideals should the organization maintain? The board defines the appropriate organizational target or outcome that, when accomplished, represents success for the organization.

Second, the board *protects* the organization by establishing boundaries that, when respected by the executive director and staff, result in the safe operation of the organization and help secure its long-term success. The boundaries are expressed as policies that start out broadly and can be narrowed with more detail to any level that the board chooses. In the end, the board's boundary statements become monitoring tools the board uses to ensure that the organization is safe and successful. These boundary reviews also provide some of the structure for board meetings throughout the year. Common boundary statements relate to the treatment of clients, staff, and volunteers, to financial planning and management, to risk management, and to compensation and benefits. The board creates and monitors boundaries that are appropriate to the organization and its work.

Third, the board *enables* the work of the organization through advocacy, resource development, and role discipline. Board members *advocate* for the organization through their own networks of professional, civic, and personal contacts. Every conversation they have is an opportunity to advocate for the needs and mission of the organization. They represent the organization to every person with whom they interact. Because of the board members' influence, the organization is made visible to everyone the members know or to who knows them. Of course, this means that each board member must clearly understand the work of the organization.

Moreover, each board member's advocacy relationship is also a *resource development* opportunity. This does not mean that each conversation needs to end with an *ask*. But it does mean that board members should always be listening for possible connections between the needs of the organization and the talents and resources of their contacts. There will be times when an *ask* is appropriate, and it may or may not be the role of the board member to make the request. In some cases, it may be more appropriate for the board member to refer the contact to the executive director or to someone else on the organization's staff so that individual can make the request.

Boards also enable the organization by maintaining *discipline* to their proper role. As soon as boards begin to veer from their directing, protecting, and enabling role, they risk disabling, or at least complicating, the efforts of the staff. Board members are often tempted to wander into leading, managing, and accomplishing roles. They will, however, enable the staff more by staying out of those areas and restricting themselves to the roles of directing, protecting, and enabling.

The Executive Director and Staff Roles

For many governance models, including Carver's Policy Governance, the executive director's role is uncharted territory. But for Aligned Influence, it is as critical as the board's role. According to Aligned Influence, the executive director's role is to lead, manage, and accomplish the work of the organization.

Given that the board defines the strategic *what* of the organization, the executive director and his staff define the tactical *how* to accomplish the strategic *what*. The executive director is empowered by the board to accomplish the work of the organization in any way she sees fit within the boundaries set by the board. And the executive director does this through short-term and long-term organizational plans that apply to her work and that of her staff. In other words, the executive director is to *lead*.

To this point, I have used the word *influence* as a substitute for the words *lead* and *leadership*, and when I have used leadership terms, I have used them in the context of the ecosystem of influence, pointing out that board members, executives, and many others within an organization exercise leadership—that is, influence—whether or not their specific job title indicates this. While I do not intend to leave that understanding behind, when I talk about the leadership role of the executive director, I have in mind a typical way that his leadership-influencing role is carried out at the executive level. So in this sense, when I talk about the executive's leadership, I am referring to leading through *future-focused planning*.

This level of leading considers how the organization must orient itself and change to accomplish the work of the organization in the context of shifting challenges and opportunities. Some of these shifts come from the board making changes in organizational direction, while other shifts may issue from economic, social, legal, and even environmental changes coming from government, the marketplace, and the community within which the organization's work is done. Executive directors lead by figuring out how to navigate these waters so they can keep their organizational ship afloat and pointed in the best direction.

Executive directors also *manage*. People often confuse leadership and management. Even the literature on leadership frequently merges and confuses these two influencing roles. Leadership and management are both important, but they are not the same. As I see it, leadership is *future focused* while management is *present focused*. The task of managing relates to how the work of the organization must be structured to ensure it is accomplished on time, on budget, and on target. Management involves establishing and maintaining the systems and processes that staff use to do the work of the organization.

The executive director must be aware of and honest about his strengths and weaknesses in these tasks of leading and managing. It is a rare person who can do both jobs well, and no one lacks weaknesses in either area. Consequently, the executive director needs to surround herself with staff and volunteers who can use their strengths to reduce, if not eliminate, the liabilities of her weaknesses while also freeing up her strengths and the benefits they bring.

Under Aligned Influence, the executive director is also tasked with *accomplishing* the work of the organization. She uses the strategic direction and operational boundaries provided by the board to create tactical plans, operational policies, and procedural guidance that ensure the organization will accomplish its work and maintain its integrity.

Executive directors and staff operate the organization, accomplish the goals established by the board, and provide the board with monitoring information. Executive directors operate the organization within the context of the board's governing policies by establishing operational policies, structuring resource development efforts, hiring and managing personnel, and establishing processes and procedures by which products or services are consistently delivered. They structure the organization internally so the day-to-day tasks of keeping the organization moving forward are established and well managed. Internal staff may perform some of these tasks, while other tasks may be outsourced (for example, staff may hire an accounting firm for accounting tasks). Regardless of who does the work, the executive director is the one ultimately responsible for the accomplishment of these operational tasks.

The executive director's role does not conflict with the board's role but rather complements it. For example, an educational foundation raises and distributes funds to the educational institution they are aligned with. A food bank raises funds, procures food donations, and then develops processes and procedures for distributing that food appropriately. An affordable-housing organization's work is building and remodeling housing that can be made available to families at a reachable cost. In all of these examples, the board defines the strategic *what*, and the executive director and his staff define and accomplish the tactical *how*, focusing on doing the programmatic work of the organization.

As part of their accomplishing role, executive directors are responsible for providing the board with the information they need to appropriately monitor the organization. Boards typically monitor each of their protective policies once a year. With ten to twenty policies, the board reviews at least one policy per month, and the executive director provides operational reports for this process. Boards often perform external monitoring on some of the protected areas. In these cases, the staff will work with an external auditor to provide audit information. By providing such information to the board, executive directors are demonstrating to what degree they are accomplishing the work of the organization.

The Union of Roles

In Aligned Influence, the board and the executive not only collaborate. They also align their roles. Let's return to the gears illustration again.

The traditional nonprofit approach, illustrated by the gears-separated illustration, is a governance model that has the board on one side and the executive director and his team on the other side (see Figure 2). While the board and director need to collaborate to move their organization forward, their governance model actually frustrates their ability to work together. The executive gear and the board gear try to link through policy documents and reports, but their paper link does not foster a genuine ability to get and stay in sync. They remain apart, turning often in competing directions and at different speeds.

The overlapping gears approach doesn't fare any better (see Figure 3). The executive and his board trip over one another more than they collaborate. Competitions for power, mistrust, and suspicion are easily bred in this model.

In Aligned Influence, we have an interlocking gears model:

Figure 6

Each gear has its own integrity, its own function, and yet both major influencer gears are clearly running in sync with each other. Through this governance model, organizations can achieve the needed collaboration between the board and the executive. Collaboration requires alignment and that's what Aligned Influence provides. Specifically, here's what I mean.

The board and the executive unite and align in two essential ways: vertically and horizontally. *Vertically*, the board's role of *directing, protecting,* and *enabling* is different from the executive director's role of *leading, managing,* and *accomplishing.* The organization depends on the board to carry out its role fully and functionally, as it depends on the executive director to fulfill his role.

Moreover, under Aligned Influence, the board actually has the task of *enabling* the organization—a task never assigned or addressed in other governance models. Even the tasks of directing and protecting, while discussed in Policy Governance under different terminology, are understood in Aligned Influence within the larger ecosystem of influence that exists in an organization—a holistic approach utterly absent in Policy Governance. So on the vertical viewpoint, Aligned Influence has a more comprehensive understanding of the board and its influence than other governance models do.

Regarding the *horizontal* relationship between the board's and executive's roles, many of the governance models have nothing substantial to say. But in Aligned Influence, the horizontal relationship between these distinct roles brings a different dimension and set of opportunities to consider. Under Aligned Influence, the board's directing role and the executive's leading role, while distinct, are also complementary and united (see chapter 8). Directing and leading are both future focused, so they work for the organization's future but in different ways. For instance, the board influences what service, product, or value is to be created by the organization, while the executive influences how that service, product, or value should be created. Both the board and the chief executive influence the organization's future, and both can do so without competing with the other. Collaboration, not competition, is the design that leads to organizational health and success. Influences are aligned rather than pitted against each other.

Aligned Influence also sees and develops the complementary relationship between the board's role of protecting and the executive's role of managing (see chapter 9), and between the board's role of enabling and the executive's role of accomplishing (see chapter 10). In broad brushstrokes, the board *protects* by defining and monitoring operational boundaries in key operational areas, while the executive director *manages* by establishing operational policies and procedures to ensure compliance with the operational boundaries that the board has defined. Furthermore, the board *enables* by creating and utilizing relationships to advocate for and develop resources for the organization, while the executive director *accomplishes* by creating products, services, or value in alignment with the board's direction. So Aligned Influence identifies, describes, and encourages the alignment between the ordered pairs of directing and leading, protecting and managing, and enabling and accomplishing.

It is essential that boards and executives respect one another's different roles and not venture in to roles that do not belong to them—this is the vertical side of the relationship between them. On the other hand, boards and executives also need to understand, appreciate, and cooperate with one another in those roles that complement each other and work most effectively together, which is the horizontal side of their relationship. Respecting one another's roles, disciplining themselves to stay within their respective roles, and yet uniting together on those roles that are aligned with each other will enable boards and executives to pull their organization together in a united way and not in competition with one another. Maintaining the horizontal and vertical sides of their relationship will bring boards and executives the organizational health and success they all want. Achieving this relationship between boards and executives is what Aligned Influence is about.

The Benefits of Aligned Influence

As the rest of the book unfolds, you will find that the benefits of Aligned Influence are many. Here I want to take some time to highlight several of these.

Provides a Holistic Approach to Organizational Development

Aligned Influence provides a mechanism for organizational development, not simply board development or only executive development. While the board's role and responsibilities are spelled out, so are those of the executive director and his entire staff. Engagement within the board, between the board and the executive director, between the board and the staff, and between the executive director and his staff are also appropriate subjects for explanation and discussion within Aligned Influence. When all is said and done, this model helps all within an organization to understand their role and how it aligns with the roles of others and how they contribute to the organization's work and success.

Embraces the Ecosystem of Influence

Aligned Influence helps organizations understand, work with, direct, and shape the ecosystem of influence within them. The lack of understanding in this critical area generates a host of problems that undermine and frustrate an organization's health and success (see part I).

Clarifies Roles

Aligned Influence provides clarity about everyone's role in areas that have frequently been in question. In areas like planning, budgeting, and development, boards and executives now understand that they are both participating in these tasks rather than competing for control over them. For example, in budgeting, boards define what needs to be accomplished and create boundaries that keep budgets and the budgeting process on track, while executives create budgets that support their programmatic efforts to accomplish that work and comply with those boundaries. Budgeting is not the responsibility of only the board or only the executive; their roles are aligned in the process.

Also, Aligned Influence addresses the executive director, not just the board. And the model provides for active participation in the work of the organization for both the board and the executive director. No one is left out. Everyone is active. And because each of the roles is clearly assigned, articulated, and aligned, board members and executives alike know what to do, why they are doing it, and how they are uniquely benefitting the direction and work of the organization. They move the organization ahead together, united and confident.

Expands Roles

Aligned Influence moves boards beyond defining the ends and limiting the means of an organization. The model expands the role of the board to enablement, adding that to its directing and protecting roles. And it shows how each of the board's three roles lines up and works with the three roles of the chief executive. So as the board directs, the chief executive in complementary fashion leads. As the board protects, the executive's role of managing is in alignment with the board's protecting role. And as the board enables the organization, the executive works to accomplish the work of the organization, which links with the board's enabling role.

Expanded roles.

Aligned roles.

Roles that engage and bring new significance and meaning to boards and executives alike.

This is what Aligned Influence accomplishes.

Increases Board Involvement

Aligned Influence opens the way for the board to engage more in the work of the organization but still in an appropriate way. The board remains disciplined by staying out of the executive director's role of accomplishing the work of the organization. On the other hand, the board now assumes the defined role of enabling the work of the organization. Board members enable this work through advocacy, resource development, and role discipline.

Avoids Damaging Competition

Aligned Influence acknowledges and surfaces the potential and actual competition for power in an organization. It addresses this problem by seeking to understand the ecosystem of influence within an organization and by clearly defining the roles for both the board and the executive director and aligning those roles so competition can be set aside and avoided.

So, according to Aligned Influence, who leads your organization? When leadership is understood as influence, the board and the executive both lead your organization but in distinctive and unique ways that align their influence rather than generate a competition for power between them.

Emphasizes People Over Policies

I have not talked much about policies yet (see chapter 11), but I have already pointed out that, under Aligned Influence, policy statements are not the end-all of what the board or the executive does. Policies are a means to an end, not an end in themselves. They are important tools people can use in finding and forming solutions, but policies are not solutions themselves. On their own, they do not accomplish anything. They are simply words on paper. The doers are people. People do the work, including creating the documents used in an organization to help give it direction and protection. Aligned Influence puts the emphasis where it belongs—on people, not policies, yet without ignoring the latter.

Provides Visibility

Aligned Influence provides visibility for the executive and staff into the board's role and vice versa. Everyone knows each other's role in the organization. This visibility leads to a better understanding of and appreciation for each other's roles, and this improves each person's ability to comply with and be successful in his or her own roles.

Creates a Clear Structure for Professional Development

Aligned Influence provides a structure for professional development for the board, the executive director, and other influencers in the organization. Board members can develop the abilities needed to direct, protect, and enable the work of the organization, while executive directors can develop the abilities to lead, manage, and accomplish that work. Every board member and executive director is "wired" to be better at one of their roles than the others. So professional development should include board members and executives exploring and sharpening their own skill set, while also learning more about how they can work in concert with others in the organization to ensure the entire team's success.

What's Ahead

Now it's time to launch into the details of the Aligned Influence model. In the next chapter, I will focus on the board and its yoked role of directing, protecting, and enabling. In the ensuing chapter, I will turn my attention to the executive's part of the yoke of leading, managing, and accomplishing. These two chapters will treat each of these defined roles vertically. In other words, I will consider what the board does without linking it to what the executive does, and I will do the same with the executive's role. After that, I will treat boards and executives in relationship to one another—that is, horizontally. I will walk through how the board's directing and the executive's leading are united, then the union of the board's protecting and the executive's managing, and finally the union of the board's enabling and the executive's accomplishing.

Rounding out this part of the book I will explain the three policy sets of maturing organizations, and the kind of board members and executives one needs to fulfill the roles Aligned Influence assigns to them. The last section of the book will focus on the steps needed to make Aligned Influence the guiding light of your organization.

Theory is one thing. Application another. We cannot apply what we do not know. But knowledge alone does not bring about change. So once I have explained Aligned Influence in detail, I will show you what it takes to make it a reality.

7

Boards That Direct, Protect, and Enable

So what should a board do?

Imagine a bare, flat piece of land that needs to be properly prepared to sustain landing aircraft. Among the required basics is laying down pavement that can *enable* the planes that will land there. The pavement will need lines painted on it that will provide *direction* to the planes so their pilots know where to land. Along both sides of the pavement, lights will need to be installed to provide proper boundaries that will help *protect* planes as they land. This is analogous to what boards do for their organizations. They set the *direction* (paint the lines) the organization needs to follow; they establish *protections* (install the landing lights) to help keep the organization within safe boundaries; and they *enable* (lay down durable pavement) to sustain the organization over the years and challenges to come.

Let's take a closer look at each of these defining board functions.

Boards Direct

A board decides what their organization is to accomplish—the targets their organization needs to hit. This is the big-picture role. What should the organization do? What will be its work? Put another way, establishing an organization's direction is a future-oriented task. When board members do this, they are saying, "Here is where we want our organization to go." They are pointing the way. Or, as the airport analogy puts it, the board is painting the lines for the executive director and staff to follow for landing the organizational plane.

Directing the organization involves determining the product, service, or value that the organization will provide and the ideals that should be maintained in the process. The *product* could be anything from soup to satellites, wheat to warehouses, houses to Hummers, cake to computers. The *service* may be repairing refrigerators or restoring marriages, or feeding starving animals or building and paying for homes for individuals or families who cannot afford them. The *value* might be increasing a community's awareness of homelessness or homeland-security needs, or highlighting educational achievements, needs, or issues, or keeping state representatives informed of various local, county, and even state-wide concerns. Whatever the product, service, or value, the board identifies it and establishes it as the *what* for the organization to accomplish.

To provide this direction, board members need to do several things. One, they need to identify who they are responsible to. They need to ask themselves, "Who cares that our organization exists? Who has a stake in our success?" Of course, the staff and leadership in an organization are stakeholders, so they form part of the answer here. But who along with them cares about your organization and its success? Community leaders? Other for-profits and nonprofits that depend in some way on what you do? Political officeholders? Certain consumer groups? Whoever they are, a board needs to identify them—all of them. Some will not be as obvious as others. If you are a board member, you will need to move beyond the confines of the boardroom and talk to others outside the organization, ask them questions, and listen to their answers to learn who those are who care about your organization and its success.

Once a board has identified who cares, they need to learn from these stakeholders. Find out what they have to tell you about your organization and why it matters to them. Discover what they have to say about what your organization currently does and what it needs to do to better serve them or others who also rely on your organization.

Some of these stakeholders may also help you see what challenges are coming, which can give you a head start for considering what you as a board may need to do to address those challenges in your organization. Do you need to revise the organizational direction you have given? Does your organization need to be reshaped in some way? If so, what direction can you give as a board to paint the way for this to happen? Stakeholders can also speak to opportunities your organization may have—opportunities to expand your market share, your product or service offerings, your customer or client base, your influence, and even your innovation potential.

To direct their organization, board members also need to understand what the organization's work is or is supposed to be. This requires having some knowledge of the work to be achieved, what similar organizations are doing to accomplish this kind of work, and how the work gets done. Board members do not have to be experts at accomplishing the work; this will be a need for the organization's executive director and her staff. But board members need to understand enough about the work in order to provide direction for it.

Another aspect of the board's directing work is the board directing itself. Self-governance is critical to the board accomplishing its own work. The board needs to organize its work for the short term and the long term. To accomplish this, the board needs to develop and maintain its own annual calendar. The board's calendar is not the executive's. The board's calendar needs to set the days and times and deadlines for accomplishing its work of directing, protecting, and enabling.

Boards Protect

Along with directing the organization, boards set boundaries to protect the organization. Just as aircraft needs to know where the edges of the runway are, so an organization needs to know the lines it should not cross as it seeks to accomplish the work set by the board. These protections are established to ensure the safe operation of the organization, to protect its reputation, to provide its standards, and to secure its long-term success. They are expressed as policies that start out broadly and can be narrowed with more detail to any level that the board chooses. Through this protection role, the board shares responsibility for the operations of the organization, and it does so by setting the standards the organization should follow while carrying out its work.

Before I say more, I want to acknowledge the work of John Carver in this area. What he has said about protective boundaries is important and still needed in policy-governance discussions. In fact, his work on policy sets centered on governance ends and executive limitations has laid the foundation for subsequent documentary work in organizations. So, some of what I say in this section (and in chapter 11 on policy sets) builds on his work.

The board lays down protections in the form of statements that tell the executive director what *not* to do, not what to do. They are negative statements, not positive ones. Protection statements never appear in the affirmative—"the executive director shall"—but always in the negative—"the executive director shall not or shall not fail to." Limits set the boundaries for the organization's work; they do not specify how the work must be done. Limiting statements say, "Beyond this point you shall not go." And they assume that within the boundaries set, organizational leadership has a great deal of freedom to plan, budget, produce, earn, and do whatever else is needed to accomplish what the board has *directed* them to do.

The board, for example, in thinking about the financial side of the organization, may form a protective statement around liabilities: "The executive director shall not allow organizational liabilities to be twice as much as its assets." The board does not specify exactly what the ratio of liabilities to assets should be. Instead, the board places a limit that says beyond this you should not go.

Around the area of financial accountability, the board could establish this boundary statement: "The executive director shall not fail to have an external auditor review the books less than once every two years." To satisfy this, the executive director may actually have an independent audit of the books once a year rather than every two years. But note that the board sets the boundary—a boundary in which the director has room to work in the way that fits within the board's established limit and what she deems appropriate for the organization she leads.

Consider another example based on human resources. The board might establish a protection that stipulates that the executive director shall not operate without written personnel policies. Notice that the board does not compose the personnel policies to be used; instead the board ensures that such policies will be drafted and enacted. Of course, the board can put more protections around such policies. For example, the board could state that the executive director shall not discriminate in hiring practices according to ethnicity, gender, and so on. The board could also say that the executive director shall not fail to establish a process for effectively handling conflict escalation and resolution. But how this should be carried out is left to the discretion of the executive director.

To establish protective policies, board members need to understand what should be protected and why. This requires that board members know enough about each of the areas of an organization needing protection—for example, human resources, compensation and benefits, finances, legal needs, property, and client relations. Members need to understand these various aspects of the organization, perhaps even know them well enough to run them themselves. But they must have the discipline to stay out of accomplishing the work that must be done in operational areas.

Boards set the boundaries of protection; boards do not step in to accomplish the work of the organization. The latter is the work of the executive director and his staff. Boards tell the director, "Do all you need and want, but do it within the boundaries we have set." Boards should not supplant or subvert the director by coming in and doing the work—*any* of the work—that he is hired to do.

Boards Enable

Once the board has laid out the organization's *direction* and established the needed *protections*, its work is not done. Of course, the board needs to monitor the executive director and the organization's progress toward accomplishing its work. Directions and protections need follow-up and accountability. But beyond this, what can the board do?

Under Aligned Influence, plenty. The board's added *do* role is to *enable* the executive director, her staff, and the organization. By enable I mean that a board should advocate for the organization, seek additional resources for the organization, and maintain discipline regarding its role in the organization. Much of this enabling role actually occurs outside the boardroom.

Advocacy and Resource Development

I urge board members, as part of their enabling work, to wear their organization on their lapels. Wherever they go, whomever they speak to, whatever they are doing, they should act as their organization's most important advocates. They keep their eyes and ears open for opportunities, individuals, resources—anything and anyone who can help move the organization forward. They serve as their organization's roving representatives.

I serve on the board of Habitat for Humanity. In that capacity, I wear a Habitat pin to civic functions I attend. It doesn't matter if Habitat is the focus of that civic event. What matters is what that pin provokes. People see it, then ask me questions about Habitat and my role there, and they even give me testimonials about how Habitat has served their community. Sometimes their comments reveal misunderstandings about Habitat that I can then clear up for them. This line of communication also provides me with the opportunity to ask them questions—questions that could generate answers that tip me off to how this person might be able to help Habitat in some way.

During one such encounter, a world-renowned documentary filmmaker ended up offering his services to film Habitat at work in building a home for a needy family. Since its production, this film has been used in numerous ways to educate countless individuals, groups, and organizations about Habitat's work, which has led to other individuals and groups coming alongside Habitat to offer money, expertise, and even promotional opportunities to further the organization's efforts. Advocacy led to resources that benefitted the organization and led to its ongoing sustaining power and influence. This is the kind of paving work that keeps an organization moving ahead into the future.

If you are a board member, you have many opportunities to promote the organization that you serve. In most cases, you will be able to do this in casual conversations. Sometimes a speaking engagement might come available or perhaps a blogging invitation. Whatever the venue, you can make your organization visible. You can say to someone, "Did you know I am on the board of XYZ organization? May I take a few minutes to tell you what we do and explain some of the challenges we face?" Few people will turn you down. And with these advocacy opportunities, you will often uncover resources your organization will be able to use to further nurture and sustain its growth. You may be able to bring into your organization

- talent it needs;
- a consultant who can show how to meet present or looming challenges;
- a publicity or marketing expert who can take your organization to the next level of market exposure;

- a financial resource that can provide needed funds for planned growth;
- someone who would make a great board member to replace a member who will be leaving;
- a proven coach or mentor to come alongside your chief executive;
- a builder who can provide a better way to meet, even exceed, your organization's structural needs and dreams.

The list of potential resources you can find goes on and on—if you as a board member will advocate for your organization at every opportunity afforded you.

Role Discipline

Another way a board can enable its organization is by sticking to its assigned roles as a board. As long as board members *direct, protect,* and *enable* rather than slip into the executive director's roles of *leading, managing,* and *accomplishing,* they will do their part in sustaining the health of the organization they serve. And they can accomplish this work without moving over into the executive's work.

Whenever a board is tempted to drop down into an operational issue, I ask them to pose this question: What is it about the direct, protect, and enable policies currently in place that are not robust enough to address the issue you now face? By addressing this question, the board can engage the issue while remaining disciplined to their role.

Back to the Airport

Boards do not land the organizational plane. On the other hand, without what they do, the executive director and his staff could not land the plane either. Boards make it possible for employees to accomplish the work of the organization. They lay the needed pavement (the foundation that enables), they paint the lines on the runway (the direction needed), and they set up the lights to show the runway's boundaries (the protections within which organizational flight will stay safe and secure). Then, and only then, will the executive director and his staff have all they need to succeed in landing the organizational plane.

Figure 7

Now it's time to delve into what executives do under Aligned Influence.

8

Executives Who Lead, Manage, and Accomplish

Under Aligned Influence, executives do not perform the actions assigned to the board of directors. Executives lead, manage, and accomplish the work of the organization. Using the flight analogy from the previous chapter, they are the ones who get inside the cockpit of the organization, fly the plane, and land it. The chief executive officer and her team of fellow executives do this by working through and relying on their paid staff, volunteers, and many others associated with their organization.

More specifically, the executive director uses the board's strategic direction and operational boundaries to create tactical plans and operational policies that ensure the organization will accomplish its work and maintain its integrity. Executive directors and staff operate the organization, accomplish the goals established by the board, and provide the board with monitoring information. Executive directors also operate the organization within the context

121

of the board's governing policies by establishing operational policies, structuring resource development efforts, hiring and managing personnel, and establishing processes and procedures by which products or services are consistently delivered. In short, executive directors structure the organization internally so the day-to-day tasks of keeping the organization moving forward are established and well managed.

Internal staff may accomplish some of these tasks, while other tasks are done through outsourced services (for example, staff may hire an accounting firm for accounting tasks). Regardless of who does the work, these operational tasks are the executive director's responsibility.

In other words, the executive director flies and lands the organizational plane by *leading*, *managing*, and *accomplishing* the work of the organization. These three roles are quite different from those of the board, and yet they also complement the board's roles. The executive director's task does not conflict with the board's but aligns with it. Moreover, what the executive is supposed to do is not more or less important than what the board does. The executive and the board perform complementary and equally beneficial roles in and for the organization they serve and for those who depend on their organization and its work.

As we did with boards, let's take a closer look at each of the executive's central roles and responsibilities as established under Aligned Influence.

Executives Lead

The direction that the board hands down to the executive tells him *what* the organization needs to accomplish. The *what* can be broad, lacking few if any specifics, or it can be laid out in a fair amount of detail. Either way, the board's direction gives the executive the target to hit, but it does not tell him how to hit it. For the *what* to be achieved, the *how* has to be developed.

How will the organization accomplish what the board has defined for it? That task is the executive's. He must articulate how the board's direction will be accomplished. He must decide how to fly and land the organizational plane. In other words, since the board defines the strategic *what* of the organization, the executive director and his staff define the tactical *how* to accomplish the strategic *what*. This does not mean that the executive director is relegated to the mundane. Rather, he is empowered by the board to accomplish the work of the organization in any way he sees fit—as long as that occurs within the boundaries the board has established.

Now, the board's direction leaves a great deal of room for movement. The board does not answer a host of questions— questions that require specific answers about a number of critical matters: for example, what the organization's resources are; the resources it does not have but may have access to; the experience, talents, weaknesses, and strengths of the organization's workers, from its upper echelon of leaders to its middle managers and those they oversee; the organization's past successes and failures; and the financial viability of the organization and the financial strength it needs to move forward. The areas of focus and concern can seem endless, as can the questions that need to be answered.

Executives cannot find out the answers to their questions on their own. In fact, they cannot get the organizational directives done on their own either. They need help, and this includes listening to what others in and outside the organization have to say.

So, to get the job done, executives need to know where they are going and the shape of the organization they are tasked to lead.

I argued earlier that leadership, at its core, is influence. A board tasks the executive with leading the organization forward. But the executive cannot do this alone. She must find ways to influence the organization's other executives, managers, and fellow workers to follow her lead and use their influence to contribute to accomplishing the organization's goals. The more effective her leadership, the more of the work will get done and get done well. Without influential leadership, organizations flounder, workers lose their focus and drive, targets are routinely missed, resources are misused and dwindle, and customers start looking elsewhere to get their needs and wants fulfilled. How executives use their influence to lead has a huge impact on organizational success and health.

Executives must lead and lead well. Entire books have been written on what all this entails, so I can only scratch the surface here. I will lay out some leadership essentials that are particularly important for understanding and applying the role of executive leadership in the Aligned Influence model.

Leaders Must Know Where They Are Going

The executive must understand where she is supposed to take the organization. Under Aligned Influence, the board's role is to set this direction. So the executive needs to learn what the board has laid out. Knowing the particular industry in which the organization operates is valuable, even essential, but not enough on its own. Even the executive's past success in that industry is inadequate, though worthwhile. The executive must seek to understand the board's direction for the organization she leads. She must know what her target is before she can figure out how to hit it. Changing the metaphor, you cannot land a plane on a runway you cannot see. And if you land the plane going the wrong way on the runway, you may crash it.

Leaders Must Know What Not to Do

The executive must also understand what protections—the not-to-dos—that the board has established for the organization. The protections exist for the sake of the organization, those who work for it and in it, those who invest in it, and the customers it serves. The executive who knows these protections and works within them will better serve the organization he leads. (For much more on this, see chapter 11.)

Leaders Must Lay Plans for Changing Times

Along with following the board's directives and working within its protections, the executive leads his organization by planning for how the organization's tactics, methods, and efforts need to change as the environment in which it operates changes. The board's focus is on the *future* of the organization, looking to what the organization should strive to accomplish. The executive, on the other hand, needs to lean into *how* the organization can accomplish the goals the board has laid out, and how that needs to happen now as well as into the not-yet. Present conditions change. Markets shift. Customer wants and even some needs grow or decrease or even fall away. An executive needs to stay in touch with the investors and clients served by his organization so he can guide it into serving them better.

Leaders Must Form Strategic Partnerships

Executives also need to partner with other organizations in the community to assist them and their organization. For example, a publishing company needs to work with printing companies, wholesalers, retail outlets, media, and even other publishers in foreign countries to turn a book into a successful sales product. An animal shelter for dogs and cats needs to have partners in local animal patrol, various civic organizations, city leaders, and animal care advocates to effectively serve the community. And for every organization—whether a publishing company, an animal shelter, a manufacturer, a church, or a school—its partners will help it better understand the role it plays and its importance to those it serves.

Executives Manage

Along with leading, executives *manage* the work of the organization. Leadership and management are often confused. *Leadership* is future focused and considers how the organization must change to accomplish its work in the context of shifting challenges and opportunities. *Management*, on the other hand, is focused on the present, and it relates to how the work of the organization must be structured now to ensure it is accomplished on time, on budget, and with excellence. Both leadership and management are important, and often an executive director is stronger in one area than the other. But to be successful, she must focus on both leadership and management. And she must realize what her strengths and weaknesses are in each area, and then surround herself with staff and volunteers who can help her overcome her areas of weakness, not just for her sake but also for the organization's benefit.

Leaders manage in at least two essential ways. One way is by ensuring that sufficient policies, procedures, training, and supervision are in place so that the organization's work can get done in a timely, effective, and cost-beneficial way. It takes more than people working to complete the necessary tasks. There must be clear and adequate policies and processes developed and documented. There must be training available, not just for new hires but also for addressing adjustments in the marketplace that require the acquisition of new knowledge and skills for those doing the work. The supervision of personnel is also critical. The best supervisors are those who know when to be hands-on and when to back off, when to apply more pressure and when to relax it, when to push and when to stop to celebrate. The most effective executives manage the organization's structure. They know it and understand it, and they keep their eyes on it to make sure it matures and functions well.

The second critical way executives manage is by ensuring that all of the day-to-day tasks and responsibilities are completed and completed consistently over time. The larger an organization, the more difficult this part of managing becomes. An executive in a large organization will likely need to have some trustworthy and accomplished people in place who will report to her, telling her more than what they think she wants to hear, telling her what she needs to hear about how well the various divisions and departments are accomplishing their work. She will need to work with other executives and managers to update procedures, solve employee problems, and whatever else needs to be resolved. Many executives refer to this kind of work as putting out fires. All who work in for-profits and nonprofits know that flare-ups occur; they're even expected. And some of these fires can be put out fairly easily and quickly. Some, however, can turn into major burns, and some of these may require the direct involvement of the chief executive. This is all part of the executive's management role.

Executives Accomplish

Executive directors and their staff are also responsible for accomplishing the work authorized by the board. For example, an independent school needs to understand why it is choosing to be independent. What will it focus on that will differ from what the public schools offer? Who are the people it will serve, and what are these clients willing to pay for? Are they looking for a faith-based environment and curriculum? Do they want a different student discipline approach? Perhaps they need to have a place where certain needs are better met for students who have autism or face other similar issues. Or consider a city. Civic leaders need to decide what is going to be unique about their city. What is it going to be known for? And what can be done to attract developers and employers to their city? Another example is an investment company. It needs to understand what their clients want from them. Is it liquidity? A high return on their investment? Safety for their finances? In all of these examples, the board defines the strategic *what* of the organization while the executive director and his staff define and accomplish the tactical *how*, focusing on doing the programmatic work of the organization.

Executive directors are also responsible for providing the board with the information it needs to appropriately monitor the organization. Boards typically monitor each of their protective policies once a year, and the executive provides operational reports for this process. Boards also often perform external monitoring on some of the protected areas. In these cases, the staff will work with an external auditor to provide the appropriate information.

The bottom line for the executive is that the work of the organization gets done. And that it gets done today, tomorrow, next week, every month, year in and year out. The board sets out the vision, and the executive accomplishes the vision. The *what* defined by the board becomes the *getting-it-done* work of the executive. In other words, the executive is the one who makes sure that the organizational plane lands properly, beneficially, and safely on the runway built by the board.

Executives accomplish the organization's work in a number of ways. They utilize the organization's structure and staff. They work to ensure that staff have the resources they need to fulfill their responsibilities and roles. Executives also strive to make sure that the structure within which the staff works supports their efforts rather than frustrates them.

Executives seek to find the right people for the right positions to fulfill the work of the organization. And then executives let those staff members execute their roles. They do not step in to do the work they have found others to do.

Upper-level executives also hold the organization's employees and volunteers accountable for the various jobs laid out for them. They may do this through lower-level executives, mid-level managers, and the like, but executive directors realize that, without accountability, the work of the organization will suffer.

Executives also seek out and bring alongside added resources they need to understand and meet the operational challenges they face. These resources may include consultants and advisors, seminars and associated materials, wise and reliable vendors, sources of professional development, and the like. Whatever the resource, executives are actively looking for the support they and their organization need.

In short, executive leaders *accomplish* the work of the organization. They do the work the board has tasked them to do. They produce and deliver the promised products and services. They meet and even exceed the expectations of their organization's stakeholders, stockholders, and donors. Executives make the intended contribution, bring about the differences that matter, and deliver the work that has a positive impact on their organization's clients and community. Executives follow through. They land the organizational plane in such a way that the board approves and their investors see that their investment was worthwhile.

9

Uniting Directing and Leading

Now that you know the three major roles of the board and the three major roles of the executive director under the Aligned Influence model, let's focus on the link between the vertical articulation of their respective roles and their horizontal alignment. In other words, let's see how the board's roles and the executive's roles complement one another.

I have already indicated which board roles align with which executive roles. The following graphic displays this:

Figure 4

The *directing* role of boards complements the *leading* role of executives. The role of *protecting* that boards perform fits well with the *managing* role that executives carry out. Finally, the board's *enabling* role pairs well with the executive's *accomplishing* role. When a board leans into its side of the yoke of directing, protecting, and enabling, and the executive director leans into his side of the yoke of leading, managing, and accomplishing, they have the alignment needed to move their organization forward, to mature it, and to see it enjoy success for years to come. How this works is what I want to explain in this chapter and the next two. It involves not just understanding what each of these roles involves—which is what I laid out in the previous two chapters—but also how these roles are actually aligned in my Aligned Influence approach. So in the present chapter, I start explaining this *how* with the first pair of aligning roles: directing and leading.

The First Pair of Aligned Union

Board members and chief executives are selected for a number of reasons, but usually numbered among them are beneficial traits, such as their ability to think creatively, communicate clearly, and create plans that positively influence and benefit the organization they serve. Board members and executives are also chosen for their knowledge and skills, their successes and connections, and many other traits and experiences they have in common. What they share unites them and provides a valuable foundation for coming together as a team to accomplish common goals.

The presence of commonalities, however, does not always lead to teamwork, much less to success. In my consulting work, I have seen shared talents, experiences, and knowledge lead to one-upmanship, stolen credit for work accomplished, sabotage attempts to gain promotions and financial gain, role boundaries violated, and a host of other problems. Commonalities alone are not enough. Distinctives need to be joined to commonalities, and differences acknowledged and utilized in the midst of all that is shared. Moreover, the ecosystem of influence of the entire organization needs to be understood and utilized effectively, from the top down. Aligned Influence realizes these needs, accommodates them, and organizes them so that distinctive roles and responsibilities and the influence of all the players involved can work together to make common cause.

In this light, let's consider the board's directing role and the executive's leading role. As board members *direct* the organization, they are most successful when they discipline themselves to using the articulated or needed skills to determine *what* the organization should accomplish and how that direction may need to change over time. Executives who *lead*, on the other hand, are most successful when they discipline themselves to using their skills to determine *how* the organization should be accomplishing those things defined by the board and how those efforts must change over time to account for a changing environment. Notice that the *what* of directing and the *how* of accomplishing both require discipline of role. Board members need to keep themselves focused on directing the organization, while executives need to maintain their role of leading the organization. Board members should not step into leading anymore than executives should venture into directing.

Aligned Influence requires that board members maintain their distinct roles while executives maintain their own distinct roles. Boundaries must be respected. Roles should not be confused, undermined, or seized. The board's influence needs to operate through their roles of directing, protecting, and enabling, while the executive director's influence needs to be channeled through his roles of leading, managing, and accomplishing. And these roles must be maintained without separation and without confusion and without the kind of competition that hinders and hurts organizations.

Of course, under Aligned Influence, the directing and leading roles are complementary and are best achieved when they are united. In fact, these two roles belong together and work well together when they are not muddled. Here's what I mean. Boards provide overall direction for the organization, a task that is future focused. Executives make plans on how to achieve the board's direction, and that too is future focused. Both the what-needs-to-be-achieved role of the board and the how-to-achieve-that role of the executive require the ability to solicit and evaluate input, synthesize data into useful information, and identify and establish new ideas. These commonalities show that the board and the executive have shared responsibility for the future of their organization.

But in so many organizations, the board and the executive director compete for who has the responsibility to secure their organization's future. This is an unnecessary and damaging feud. Under Aligned Influence, both are responsible for the organization's future but in different ways. The board is responsible for directing the organization into the future, and the executive is responsible for leading the organization into the future. There does not have to be competition over influencing the future of the organization. The board influences what service, product, or value is to be created by the organization, and the executive director influences how that service, product, or value should be created. Commonalities and distinctives are aligned and united—as long as board members stay disciplined in their directing role and the executive director remains disciplined in her leading role.

Alignment at Work

So you can better visualize what this aligned union looks like, consider the following table that compares some directing actions of the board with some leading actions of the executive director and her staff.

Aligning the Roles of Directing and Leading

The Board *Directs*	The Executive *Leads*
Is future focused	Is future focused.
Strategically thinks about how the what of the organization is changing over time.	Strategically thinks about how the how is changing over time.

The Board *Directs*	The Executive *Leads*
Identifies and defines the *whats* to be achieved.	Turns the board's *whats* into organizational *hows*.
Identifies and engages stakeholders—those who care that our organization exists.	Uses stakeholder information to contribute daily to our organization's health, stability, and success.
Maintains and strengthens relationships with our organization's key stakeholders.	Maintains and strengthens relationships with our organization's key operational partners.
Uses the relationships with key stakeholders to develop broad direction for our organization: answering who's to be served, what's to be accomplished, and which ideals to maintain.	Develops and drives the implementation of operational policies, procedures, and plans needed to accomplish our organization's work.

This table shows that the board's role of directing and the executive's role of leading go hand in hand. The big-picture work of the board is captured and made tangible by the work of the executive and her staff. What the board says should be, the executive director turns into an is-be—a present reality—that takes root, matures, and grows in the nonprofit or for-profit world. The executive builds on the board's blueprint, turning the board's designs into a work that can be seen, touched, heard, admired, and emulated. Ideas have consequences, and the board's ideas for an organization are brought from the abstract into the concrete by the executive's efforts.

Clearly, the board and executive director need one another. Like a songwriter needs a singer, a composer needs musicians, a coach needs players, and a film director needs actors, so a board needs someone to run with their direction and find ways to make it work. Likewise, singers need songwriters, musicians need composers, players need coaches, and actors need directors. So executives, employees, volunteers, and the like need overarching goals to achieve, targets to hit, dreams to follow, and visions to believe in and work toward. This is the direction that the board supplies.

Now, the best board members are those who have some expertise in how their direction can be accomplished. They could, if they wanted, do at least some of the executive's work. But under Aligned Influence, board members have the discipline not to. They stick to their *what* and leave the *how* to the executive. Here's a way to think about this.

Imagine a board that oversees several animal shelters in a city. The board members know about cats and dogs and may even have some pets at home that they care for. A few of these board members may be veterinarians. All of them know about animals, and all of them see the need for good, working animal shelters in their community. But they don't see their job as going into any of the shelters to feed, clean, medically treat, and find homes for the animals there. Rather, these board members work to articulate what these animal shelters should value, what they should aim for, what kind and level of service they should provide. The day-to-day work in each shelter is up to others to accomplish.

Similarly, the best executives have a good working knowledge of how to provide direction for their organization. If they needed to, they could develop the overall goals, values, and even philosophy for the organization they lead. But, if they are working according to the Aligned Influence model, executives stay on their side of the table and stick to their leading role. They may, on occasion, discover a *what* for the board to consider. They may even find that some of the board's direction needs greater clarity and focus and bring that to the board's attention, inviting them to address the need. But executives lead and refuse to direct. They do their job and lean on the board to perform their proper role.

Using the animal shelter example above, executive directors in charge of the shelters and who work in them with their staff are there to love the animals and carry out the board's direction in their care of the animals and in the ways they serve the community through their shelter work. These directors do not see it as their job to develop the shelters' overall target goals. Instead, they take the board's goals and strive to fulfill them in each shelter—day in and day out, year after year.

Boards and executive directors working together, uniting directing and leading, do their respective parts in setting their organization on the best path for it to grow healthy and become successful. This is the way of Aligned Influence.

10

Uniting Protecting and Managing

I worked with a company that, from the outside, seemed to be working fairly well. The employees were doing a fine job carrying out their respective tasks in human resources, information technology, accounting, and the like. Their customers were receiving high-quality products and services. The company's stakeholders were confident in the work produced and the community impact it had. But all was not right at the top of the organization.

Before I entered the picture, the company had been following Carver's Policy Governance approach. They had been trained in it, they did ongoing reading in it, they discussed it, and they sought to implement it in every prescribed way. They also had a Policy Governance expert available to help them when they needed more clarity. The board stuck to their role of defining the ends of the organization and limiting the means. They stayed out of the executive director's work. The company's executive director reported to the board monthly, and the board trusted him. Although issues in the company occasionally arose, the board trusted the executive's explanation of them and the way he said he was handling them. From the board's perspective, they had a chief executive who was in charge and was faithfully following the ends and means they had set for him.

Unknown to the board, at least at first, many employees had numerous accounts of the executive director's character-flawed mismanagement and poor leadership. And when they tried to convey these problems within the Policy Governance system, they were stonewalled, not just by the executive but by the board also. The board was more intent on protecting the company's director than the company itself.

Following some actions the employees eventually took, the board was compelled to listen to their concerns. It finally became clear to the board that something had gone horribly wrong at the top. The board had not effectively protected the company. Mismanagement had reigned, and they had protected their chief executive, not their company. Significant change was clearly needed. And when the board confronted the executive with the evidence of his mismanagement, he eventually chose to submit his resignation.

The board contacted me many weeks after all of this had occurred. I consulted with them, walked them through my Aligned Influence approach, and helped them implement it. They have been following this new path for several years now, and it has changed the company's culture from the top down.

This example makes it clear that protection and management are certainly linked. An organization poorly protected is more vulnerable to mismanagement than a well-protected organization is. Many boards have seen it as their primary job to protect the executive director. Consequently, their organizations, investors, donors, and even customers have suffered, while the executive director feels increasingly untouchable and all-powerful.

If the executive has not been the primary object of board protection, some boards have chosen to single out investors to protect. But this is also inadequate, leaving the executive and his staff in constant fear of losing their jobs to any drop in investor confidence or satisfaction. This environment encourages executives to spin information and even doctor reports that the board may otherwise view as unfavorable to their performance. It can also discourage an executive from risk-taking or, on the opposite end of the spectrum, encourage him to exercise a reckless aggression that will do anything to attempt to bolster investor satisfaction, even if that means violating board-established boundaries or commonly held moral or legal standards.

How a board protects and what or whom it chooses to protect matters, and it significantly affects how their organization is managed by their executive director.

The Second Pair of Aligned Union

Just as the board's role of *directing* is aligned with and united to the executive director's role of *leading*, so the board's role of *protecting* is united to and aligned with the director's role of *managing*. Under Aligned Influence, directing links with leading, and protecting links with managing (see Figure 4).

Directing and leading are concerned with the *future* of the organization, whereas protecting and managing deal with the *present* of the organization. Directing and leading are two distinct and complementary ways to influence the direction of the organization in terms of its goals, values, and ideals.

Protecting and managing, on the other hand, exercise influence on the operational realities of the organization. And like directing and leading, protecting and managing are distinct while also complementary.

Let's briefly recall what these two roles are before we consider how they fit together. The board's protective work should be focused on the organization as a whole, not simply on the board or the chief executive or the investors or on any other entity. The board protects the *entire* organization by establishing boundaries that, when respected by the executive director and staff, result in the safe operation of the organization and help secure its long-term success. The boundaries are expressed as policies that start out broadly and can be narrowed with more detail to any level the board chooses.

These boundary statements are expressed in the negative: "The executive shall not . . . " or "The executive shall not fail to . . . ." For example, the board could set the following boundary: "The executive officer shall not fail to protect organizational information and the technology on which it is stored as an asset of the organization." Notice that the board is not giving the executive an exact amount to keep in reserve or even what must be done to fulfill this goal. Instead, the board sets out the boundary within which the executive should operate. How that boundary statement is met is left to the executive and his staff.

Also, the board's boundary statements become monitoring tools that the board uses to ensure the organization is remaining safe and successful. These boundary reviews provide some of the structure for board meetings throughout the year. Common boundary statements relate to the treatment of clients, staff, and volunteers, to financial planning and management, to risk management, to compensation and benefits, and to information and industrial risk. Whatever they cover, boundaries are created that are appropriate for the organization and its work.

Board members are most successful when they discipline themselves to using their skills to establish boundaries to be respected by the executive. This will maintain the integrity of the organization. Boundaries communicate safety zones. They are not meant to exert arbitrary authority but to establish the boundaries in each area within which the executive has full authority to manage as he sees fit.

What the board protects, the executive director and his staff manage—and then some. The role of management includes a wide array of areas, including financial management, human resources management, risk management, process management, client-relationship management, and change management. Executive directors will be most successful when they use their skills to establish operational policies and procedures that allow the organization to complete its work and serve its clients in any way that honors the boundaries the board establishes. The executive manages through the establishment of these structuring policies and procedures. They become the executive's voice to all staff, including volunteers, to ensure that every staff member, volunteer, and client is treated consistently and that sufficient guidelines are in place to ensure that all of the administrative tasks of the organization are completed accurately and in a timely manner.

In their protecting role, the board establishes what will be protected and the protective boundaries to be set. In the executive's managing role, he has the freedom to do whatever he deems best for the organization within those established boundaries. Here is another way to visualize this in terms of how these two roles align:

Aligning the Roles of Protecting and Managing

The Board *Protects*	The Executive *Manages*
Protects the reputation of our organization.	Honors and enhances our organization's reputation by building a strong team that can effectively manage the organization and accomplish its work according to the ideals set.
Protects our organization as a whole, including its variety of outside stakeholders.	Develops a well-organized organization that consistently upholds its established ideals and delivers its goods, services, and values even above market expectations.
Sets boundaries to give the board standards by which to monitor our organization.	Views the boundaries as limits to stay within, not as directions to achieve.
Thinks about operational areas (e.g., HR, risk management, compensation and benefits) as boundaries, telling the executive what not to do, not what to do.	Creates and establishes operational policies and procedures that reflect the boundaries set by the board and effectively guide the work of paid and volunteer staff.
Serves as an internal auditor against the boundaries set.	Develops operational goals and plans to ensure that our organization is accomplishing the work above and beyond the board-established boundaries.

The Board *Protects*	The Executive *Manages*
Lays out the rules of engagement before problems arise.	At minimum, follows the board's rules of engagement while also looking for ways to provide more robust solutions to problems that arise.
Determines the appropriate level of flexibility to give the executive.	Does not work just to stay safe within the board-set boundaries but looks for ways to flourish within these boundaries; seeks to be creative.
Holds the executive accountable for meeting board-set standards.	Reports to the board as required, showing not only that my staff and I are meeting the board's standards but how we are appropriately exceeding them.

The board's boundaries do not dictate what the executive director does. Instead they provide the outlying framework within which he has a great deal of room to move, to be creative, to achieve, and to enjoy and expand his work and that of his staff and the organization.

Together, protecting and managing influence how the organization operates. They provide a safe and secure environment where the work of the organization can be carried out and flourish.

11

Uniting Enabling and Accomplishing

Kirk and Lisa have just sat through their twenty-fifth board meeting in two years. Though they usually don't get together after board meetings to talk, tonight is different. In the meeting, each noticed that the other person was doodling on one of the reports submitted to the board. Their boredom was obvious, at least to each other. So after the meeting, they checked in with each other and decided to connect at a nearby restaurant.

"I don't know how many more reports I can review and discuss," Lisa says, exasperated.

Kirk nods. "I know. I feel the same way. The organization seems to be doing fairly well, at least that's what the reports tell us. But each time I see our executive director, Katherine, she seems exhausted."

"She may be nearing burnout," Lisa says in a reflective way, "and I'm struggling over whether there's anything truly significant for the board to do."

"Well, what we do matters. We need to do our part to keep the organization and our executive on track—"

"I'm not denying that," Lisa interrupts. "But beyond reviewing reports and hearing our weary Katherine give us an overview of each of them, what is there for us to do? We have limited our involvement to means and ends—two words I tire of hearing. Now all we do is sit around a table, review and discuss reports, set our board calendar, and snack on fruit. I wanted to serve on this board because I thought I could help move the organization forward. Am I doing that? Is this what board influence looks like?"

Kirk gazes at Lisa, then stares across the room. While still looking away, he answers, "If this is how we impact the organization, I don't think I can do it much longer. I'm losing interest . . . and focus. And I'm frustrated by the restraints we're under. I can't say anymore that my work on the board has value. The board philosophy says it does, but I'm having a hard time seeing it anymore."

Lisa nods in agreement. Silence settles between them as dishes clatter while waiters and waitresses clear tables and serve new guests.

Katherine walks into her office. Another board meeting has come to an end. As usual, she and her staff prepared the needed reports, and she reviewed them with the board and answered the questions that came from the usual board members. Since the board dismissed her so they could continue their meeting, she returned to her office and remained there until the board finished their work and the members left the building. As usual, she saw them out, locked the doors behind them, and retired to her office.

She sits at her desk, noticing it is near 9:20 p.m. She swivels her chair so she can look out her third-floor office window. The evening lights glisten. The street noises are minimal, and the office is quiet.

But Katherine's thoughts are nagging. *How much longer can I keep this up? These sixteen-hour days are wearing me out. The board sits in the conference room, puts their stamp of approval on what I'm doing, and then leaves, thinking all is well and good and that they have done all they need to do. I'm running the organization, I'm promoting the organization, I'm actively protecting the organization. I am doing all the work! And I'm exhausted. Should I tell the board that I could use their help? Some of the board members have incredible skills and knowledge and connections. But they seem content to stay in their governance bubble and discuss while I run around getting the work done. I don't know how much more of this I can endure.*

Katherine knows she needs to go home, but her body feels resigned to rest in the chair while her mind slips into a weary spiral of struggle.

* * * *

Kirk and Lisa are dealing with a situation that affects countless board members in a wide variety of organizations. They have written the policies. They have established the organizational means and ends. What is left for them to do? Reading and reviewing reports appears to be practically all they do now. It's little wonder that board members start experiencing the level of boredom and frustration that Kirk and Lisa do.

On the other side of the table sits executives like Katherine. They are doing the work of the organization, and that work is weighing them down and wearing them out. Part of that work includes preparing the reports that the board requires. Then executives like Katherine see the board ask questions about the reports, review them, and occasionally challenge them, but in the end they do little more. Eventually executives start viewing their board as a monitoring obstacle to overcome rather than as a group of talented individuals there to help them and the organization move forward in healthy ways.

This scenario occurs far too often, but it doesn't have to be this way. Under Aligned Influence, Kirk and Lisa would find a to-do role for them on the board that goes far beyond evaluating reports, and Katherine would have a board clearly supporting her work in ways that really matter to her. What I'm talking about is the board role of *enabling* and the executive role of *accomplishing* and how those can be aligned for the good of all in the organization.

The Third Pair of Aligned Union

Boards *direct*, while executives *lead*.

Boards *protect*, while executives *manage*.

Boards *enable*, while executives *accomplish*.

These are the three aligned roles that unite in Aligned Influence (see Figure 4). Here I want to delve into how enabling and accomplishing link. To do that, let's return to the opening story for a moment.

Katherine was right to see that she was tasked to accomplish the work of the organization. But she felt overwhelmed in this role because her board was not coming alongside her in ways that were significant to her. Furthermore, Kirk and Lisa were right in their view of the board's work, seeing it lacking the significance they longed for it. And their notice of the toll the organization's work was taking on Katherine concerned them but left them wondering what, if anything, they could do to help, given the restrictions placed on the board.

What this story illustrates I have seen over and over again in my consulting work. Competent and experienced executives wear themselves down getting the organization's work done, while competent and experienced board members dwindle in their roles, losing interest in their work as it becomes so routine and mundane. Board members long for a to-do role that matters to the organization in more significant ways. Executives, on the other hand, wish their board members would find ways to support the organization's work while at the same time not getting tangled up in the organization's day-to-day affairs. The solution to board-member and executive longings starts with the board's enabling role and its union with the executive's accomplishing role. Put another way, the key to addressing executive exhaustion and board-member boredom is giving the board a to-do role that supports the executive's to-do role. Enabling and accomplishing do this.

Bored board members tend to leave the board on which they serve or find ways to involve themselves in organizational matters that lead to meddling and power struggles. In the process, the organization suffers, for it either loses highly skilled and experienced people or it pits them against one another. Talent brings nothing of value until it is channeled in beneficial ways.

How can the talented people serving on the board come alongside their executive director and support his work without doing his work? Policy Governance and the other board-governance models have no clear answer to this question. They either direct boards and executives to stay out of each other's way, or they confuse the roles of boards and executives to such an extent that they can easily become interchangeable and foster power struggles. Only Aligned Influence gives an answer that maintains the distinct roles of boards and executives while showing how they can unite without getting in one another's way.

If you'll recall, the board's enabling role turns board members into advocates for the needs and mission of their organization. In this role, board members work to increase the organization's visibility. In effect, they wear the organization on their sleeves wherever they go and with everyone they talk to. They increase awareness of and interest in their organization. They also keep their ears open for opportunities to link their organization with additional resources—resources that could advance the organization in any number of ways, including in its promotion, hiring needs, consulting needs, expansion into new markets, and financial-enrichment prospects.

Suppose your organization has a board of six members. Imagine setting those six members free to advocate for your organization, to remain aware of organizational needs to meet, to bring your organization more investors and donors, to be some of your organization's best promoters. These members outside the boardroom are letting everyone with whom they have a personal, professional, or civic relationship know that they are associated with your organization and ensuring these individuals are aware of your organization's challenges and opportunities. How would that benefit your organization? What kind of connections do you think your board members could make with people who could significantly contribute to your organization? What impact would that have on alleviating some of the stress your executive director and his staff experience? And if you are a board member, how much would this to-do role increase your sense of significance toward your work on the board? Would it inspire you? Energize you? Focus you in new and creative ways?

I have been delighted and amazed by the reports I've received from board members who get to work under the Aligned Influence model and play out their enabling role. They know that what they are doing matters. They see its impact on the vitality, stability, and accomplishments of their executive director and her staff. They feel a renewed sense of mission in board meetings and beyond.

For instance, Jeff King, a chairman of the board for the St. Vrain Habitat for Humanity in Colorado, says:

> From a board perspective, understanding the enablement role actually takes some of the pressure off . . . because now when I talk to somebody or when one of the other board members talks to somebody at a community event, it's not necessarily *I've got to get money out of this person for the organization,* it's just *I'm going to have a conversation with them about what Habitat does for the community.* And if that plants a seed for them to donate monies . . . , to volunteer their time, or . . . whatever that may be, wherever they feel they may be able to fit in, I think that's been a powerful piece of enablement. . . . If nothing else, I've educated them about Habitat.[25]

One executive director noticed some other benefits of this to-do role for his organization's board: "The enabling policy has given the board the job description in terms of being forward looking, mobilizing resources, building influence, advocating for the organization. And that in turn has given the board of directors . . . the ability to attract a higher caliber of individuals in the community to come on to our board [for they are] looking for a governing board to serve on."[26] In other words, along with helping the organization as a whole and providing better support to the executive, the enabling role has even attracted higher-quality and better-experienced people to search out this organization's board and voice interest in serving on it. How would you like that for your organization?

Enabling energizes board members, channeling their desire to do something into a role that benefits the work and the workers of the organization, including the executive director.

The board's *enabling* role aligns with and is complementary to the *accomplishing* role of the executive. For example, the executive and her team establish operational policies and procedures, hire new talent, and manage the work of the organization's personnel—all to ensure the consistent delivery of the organization's products and services. The executive and her staff do the work that the board has directed them to do. In the process, they surface challenges that they work to meet and opportunities that they strive to fulfill.

The board, on the other hand, supports the accomplishing work of the executive and her staff. The board does this by advocating for the organization, making it visible to others who may be able to help it, linking needed resources to it, and conveying those resources to the executive and his staff so they can incorporate them into their plans to further accomplish the work of the organization.

So the do role of enabling matches well with the do role of accomplishing. Board and executive align forces, unite to-do roles, and in the process build up the organization in ways that respect its ecosystem of influence. Everyone benefits. And the organizational load of getting things done is borne by the board and the executive but in different yet complementary ways. The following chart illuminates some of these aligned connections.

Aligning the Roles of Enabling and Accomplishing

The Board *Enables*	The Executive *Accomplishes*
Makes connections with stakeholders that help move the organization forward.	Accomplishes the intended work, meeting and exceeding the expectations of stakeholders; operationally moves the organization forward.
Advocates for the organization and its work.	Gives the board reason to advocate for the organization by driving accountability and getting things done in a balanced way (casting vision, establishing processes, inspiring staff, etc.).
Actively makes the organization visible in the community.	Highlights the organization's accomplishments. Demonstrates through the work done the value it has.
Helps fund or find people/volunteers who can help the executive accomplish her work in operations.	Brings in the right people and puts them in the right positions to fulfill the work of the organization.
Appropriately assists the executive in areas of struggle (i.e., if she doesn't grasp HR, points her to resources that can help her, but doesn't come in and take over that area of responsibility from her).	Seriously considers the board's counsel as well as seeks out additional ways to enhance strengths and compensate for professional weaknesses.

Through its enabling work, the board paves the way for the executive director and his staff to accomplish the work of the organization. And the executive's accomplishing work makes it easier for the board to highlight the organization and its positive impact in the community and beyond. The board and the executive work hand in hand to move the organization forward, meet the challenges it faces, and take advantage of the opportunities afforded it.

As with the other unions of roles, its imperative that board members discipline themselves to stay within their assigned roles of directing, protecting, and enabling, and that executives do the same with their roles of leading, managing, and accomplishing. This will alleviate role confusion and competition for influence. At the same time, exercising discipline to their roles will enable the board and the executive and his staff to pull the weight of the organization evenly and smoothly as they move the organization in its intended direction, helping it to mature, succeed, and grow with more stability. Frustration, loss of purpose, burnout, boredom, and other common organizational maladies can become rare and even eliminated when the board and the executive are yoked together in the way of Aligned Influence.

12

Aligned Leadership Roles, Committees, and Policy Sets

The alignment of board members and executives in their respective roles of influence is not the end of alignment in an organization. With these roles understood, it becomes increasingly clear how alignment can function in still more ways in an organization's ecosystem. I want to show this in three critical areas: (1) two important leadership roles at the top of an organization's structure, (2) committees set up by the board and committees established by the executive, and (3) the three essential policy sets of maturing organizations.

Aligned Leadership Roles

Every board has a chairperson, and every executive team has an executive director. These two leaders have different roles to play, and yet their roles are aligned. They also represent the two different sides of the same organization: the chairperson representing the oversight work of the board, and the executive director representing the operational work of the executive team and the rest of the staff and volunteers. These two leaders become the most important point of contact between their respective spheres of influence within their organization's ecosystem. Along with understanding and embracing their own roles of influence, they need to grasp each other's roles and how to work in union with one another. Cooperation, not competition, should characterize their relationship.

The Board's Chairperson

As the leader of the board, the chairperson needs to ensure that the board remains disciplined to its roles of directing, protecting, and enabling, and does not spill into the executive's roles of leading, managing, and accomplishing. He or she will then be protecting the board's unique contributions to the organization while also maintaining the prescribed freedom that the board has allotted to the executive director and the rest of the executive team.

The chairperson should also facilitate the work of the board. This would involve thinking about what should be on the board's annual calendar, which various agendas the board should work through, and what documents the board needs to ensure its aims for the organization and established protections are actually being achieved. The chairperson would also want to review the board's enabling work to assess whether it is producing the sought-after beneficial results. From all of this, he or she could then put before other board members a plan and schedule for reviewing and advancing the board's work in its three major areas of responsibility: directing, protecting, and enabling.

Along with ensuring board discipline and facilitating the board's work, the chairperson is the key contact between the board and the chief executive. Through the chairperson, the board speaks as one voice and the chief executive interacts with him or her.

Organizations may ask the board chairperson to add more to his or her plate of responsibilities, but the above are the essentials under the Aligned Influence approach.

The Executive Director

The lead executive of an organization carries out the board's direction, works within its protective boundaries, and draws upon its enabling connections. This leader oversees, organizes, and assigns the work that the staff will accomplish. She disciplines herself and all those on the operational side of the organization to the three roles of leading, managing, and accomplishing, and she strives to keep those roles aligned with the board's complementary roles. Moreover, as part of her work, she is the key contact between the board's chairperson and the organization's staff.

Alignment at the top of an organization will influence alignment throughout the organization and its ecosystem.

Aligned Committees

Organizations that form and utilize the work of various committees can bring them under alignment too. Committees the board establishes will assist the board in its oversight work, while committees created under the executive director's leadership will focus their attention on the operational side. Board committees will report their work to the board, and executive committees will report to the executive director or staff.

Board committees, then, will assist the board in its three roles of directing, protecting, and enabling. A board might have an executive committee that focuses its attention on preparing agendas and meeting documents so the board can accomplish their work when they convene. Another possible committee would be one that lays out succession or nominating plans for future board members. There could be a finance or auditing committee. Another committee could deal with community development or engagement in support of the board's enabling role. As long as board committees remain disciplined to serving the board in its three unique roles, they will support organizational alignment.

Likewise, the committees on the executive director's side will assist him and his staff in the unique roles of leading, managing, and accomplishing. These committees can support such departments as human resources, finances, and information technology, and they can recommend and help create new operational policies and procedures and help improve existing ones. As long as these committees remain within the bounds of leading, managing, and accomplishing, they can enhance and further the organization's alignment.

Aligned Policy Sets

An aligned organization has aligned policy sets along with aligned roles. I see three policy sets as critical to the establishment and operation of any organization, especially one that seeks to keep maturing. I will discuss each document set, explain why each matters, and show how each one fits into the Aligned Influence approach.

The Need

Many organizations, particularly nonprofits, begin with a small group of people trying to do the work of the organization while also providing oversight to it. As the organization matures, these working board members better define staff roles and divide up the tasks that need to be performed. Inevitably, the board hires new people to come in to fill more and more roles so the work of the organization gets done while the board begins to focus only on oversight. Before that oversight role becomes dominant, the board tries to accomplish the organization's work, substituting itself in place of an executive director and adequate staff hires. In the process, the board's oversight role takes a back seat. The organization's potential rate of growth is slowed, even hindered, and the organization suffers some losses as a result.

The same transition occurs in the maturation of organizational policy in most organizations. When an organization is formed, the founding members, usually with the help of an attorney, create documents that are used to establish the organization. These documents go by different names: for example, bylaws, statutory documents, constitution, charter, and commissioning documents. Often, young organizations try to use their establishing documents to govern and operate the organization and then keep doing that as the years go on. This actually stifles the organization's growth, even leading it to hit a plateau that it cannot move beyond. Until the board realizes that its establishing documents cannot function this way, the organization will not fill its potential. It may even suffer loss. This is because establishing documents are not designed to bear operational weight. They have an essential role to play, but advancing an organization's decision-making ability is beyond that role.

From my perspective, organizations that wish to mature need *three* policy sets: the establishing policies, governing board policies, and operating policies. Frequently, organizations try to use just one of these policy sets for oversight and operations. But organizations, be they for-profit or nonprofit, need all three of these policy sets because each set performs a function that the others do not.

Establishing Policies

Establishing policies are created with the assistance of an attorney. They focus on a number of factors, including:

- The original purpose an organization was established
- What the officers are
- What the officer structure is
- What the roles of the officers are
- The minimum or maximum number of board members
- The term limits for board members
- What kinds of skills should be represented on the board
- The number of votes necessary for a board decision to be considered a valid action
- The committees necessary to begin the initial work of the board
- What constitutes a quorum on the board
- Where the physical offices of the organization are
- How board vacancies will be handled
- How many board meetings there will be annually
- Whether any board meetings will be open to the public and under which circumstances
- How conflicts of interest will be handled
- How officers will be removed and under what conditions

In short, establishing policies are intended to document key facts that establish the initial organizational structure and procedures. They inform and provide a foundation for governing policies, but they are not intended to act as the sole governing policies for an organization. In fact, the establishing policies should be simple and straightforward. If they are not, then they are probably trying to do more than they should.

Governing Board Policies

The board of directors creates the governing policies document set. The board uses these policies to do the following:

- Define the strategic *what* the organization should deliver
- Establish boundaries within which the organization should operate to ensure its integrity, determine its fiduciary soundness, and define its appropriate risk tolerances
- Provide guidance for the board regarding how it will enable the work of the organization

In short, the governing policies structure the board's work of directing, protecting, and enabling. This document set does not tell the executive director or his staff how to accomplish their tasks. Rather, it gives them clear direction on what the organization is to accomplish; it establishes protective limits in key operational areas; and it lays out the roles of the board, including how the board intends to enable the work of the organization. The governing policies guide the board's work. They do not provide an operating manual for employees and volunteers who are seeking to actually accomplish what the organization has been set up to do.

The governing policy document addresses all three roles of the board. The *directing* portion of the governing policy defines who the organization will serve and what product, service, or value it will deliver. The *protecting* portion of the document establishes operational boundaries the executive and staff must respect. The boundaries are customized to the organization but commonly include statements about risk, finances, and human-resource management. The *enabling* portion of the governing policies defines to whom the organization is responsible, establishes procedures and guidelines to inform and unite the board in its work, and establishes procedures for monitoring the direct and protect portions of the governing policies. While governing policies are not operating policies, they certainly inform and influence the creation of operating policies.

Operating Policies

While attorneys create establishing policies and boards create governing policies, the executive director, often with the help of her staff and volunteers, creates the operating policies. Then the executive and the rest of the workers in the organization use the operating policies document set to guide the accomplishment of the organization's work. The board defines what that work is, but the executive director is assigned with getting that work done. Operating policies, and the procedures that accompany them, are designed to ensure that all staff stay in compliance with the board's direction and protection statements and policies. Operating policies and procedures also guide the staff in how to get the work done.

This operations document set addresses all the integrated aspects of the organization: human resources, accounting, research, operations, sales, marketing, production, delivery, and all the other departments in an organization. It also includes all the internal documents that have to do with operation, such as safety protocols, processes for how volunteers are brought on site, waivers, employment applications, disciplinary and termination protocols, compensation guidelines, and benefits offerings. Whatever forms, guidelines, restrictions, and so on that are needed to help staff to accomplish the organization's work, they become part of the operating policies package. And these policies direct the staff on how to accomplish their work in a way that aligns with the board's direction and stays within the limits laid out in the board's governing policies.

As you can see, the operations policies document set is much larger and more complex than the establishing policies or the governing policies. And it should be. Operations policies delve more deeply into the details of what it takes to make an organization run smoothly and effectively. Policies focused on personnel matters, operations, product delivery, departmental issues and processes, and so much more are needed for every organization, especially as an organization grows larger in size and strives to take advantage of more opportunities while solving increasing challenges. When these operations policies are done well, they replace confusion with clarity and mindless activity with purposeful direction.

Document Distinctives

Each policy document set has an author and an audience.

- For establishing policies, the author is the attorney, and the audience is the board.
- For governing policies, the author is the board, and the audience is the executive director and his team.
- For operating policies, the author is the executive director and anyone else he assigns to assist him, and the audience is his staff and volunteers.

The author is responsible for generating the document set, while the audience is responsible for executing the provisions laid out in the document set.

The following chart compares and contrasts the three essential document sets.

Essential Document Sets

Policy Set	Author	Audience (End Users)	Purpose
Establishing Policies	Attorney	Board of Directors	To establish the organization
Governing Policies	Board of Directors	Executive director and his or her team	To direct, protect, and enable the organization
Operating Policies	Executive Director	Staff and volunteers	To guide the leadership, management, and accomplishment of the organization's work

Each of these document sets is unique. Each plays a critical role in a healthy organization that the other document sets cannot fill. In fact, all three fit together as a system of policies that inform and act as a foundation for the next nested policy set in an ordered fashion. In other words, the creation of governing policies will require a review of the establishing policies to ensure continuity and alignment. Governing policies will also indicate a review of operational policies for continuity, alignment, and, more importantly, completeness. The existence of governing policies will often bring to light an area where important operating policies are missing. Each policy set plays an important role, and together they provide an organization with the policies it needs to develop in a healthy way and strive for success effectively and efficiently.

What Happens When . . .

Of course, many organizations do not have all three of these policy sets. Is that so bad? Can't an organization function on just one or perhaps two of these sets? What could go wrong?

Whenever I come into an organization operating on just one or two of these policy sets, it does not take long before I hear a sucking sound—a vacuum of influence. I hear board policies used to engage in operations, often through a series of amendments that attempt to turn board policies into operating policies and procedures. Or I hear establishing policies used to try to govern the organization. The lack of any of these policy sets creates a vacuum of influence and responsibility that cries out to be filled. Vacuums need to be filled and dealt with. Policy sets on their own will not solve the vacuum problem. And when one or more of the essential document sets are not in place and being used well, the sucking sound of influence will be heard and felt, and it will typically get addressed in ways that will hurt the organization, not help it.

I have also seen new and young organizations start out with haphazard operating policies that later became governance policies or at least were included in them. This tempts the board to micromanage the organization's work rather than encouraging board members to maintain their proper role of directing, protecting, and enabling the organization.

Some organizations believe they can operate on the basis of the establishing documents and perhaps a handful of governing policies. Some even think all they need are operating policies. Frankly, these organizations are deluding themselves. For instance, while a business or ministry with a very small number of staff or volunteers may be able to function with a handful of verbal or written operating policies, such organizations are much better served if they do the work of creating establishing policies, governing policies, and operating policies. With these sets in place, they will have the documentation they need to grow and sustain themselves well into the future.

Establishing policies are not governing policies or operating documents.

Governing policies are not establishing or operating documents.

And operating documents are not establishing or governing policies.

Each policy set fills a critical organizational need. And with any of them lacking in an organization, their absence causes a vacuum of influence that invites boards to be involved in operational issues and staffs to become involved in oversight issues. Neither bodes well for an organization's health and success.

Which of these policy sets does your organization have in place today? How is this situation working out for your organization?

Of course, policy sets are not enough on their own to mature an organization. You must have the right people in place. That's the focus of the next chapter.

13

Selecting the Board and Executive

S uppose you are on the ground floor of establishing an organization. You know you want to create an organization that will have the complexity of a board and a chief executive officer and his or her staff. You have done your homework on how to do this, and now you are ready to start the selection process for board members and the executive director. How can your knowledge of Aligned Influence help you? Let's start first with the qualifications for a board member.

Choosing Board Members

In light of Aligned Influence, choosing board members is fairly straightforward. Your organization will need to find board members who have the ability to understand the direct, protect, and enable roles; have the skills to implement those roles; and have the commitment to work within them. Put another way, the right board member is one who is equipped to direct without leading the organization, to protect without managing the organization, and to enable without accomplishing the work of the organization.

Direct Rather Than Lead

According to Aligned Influence, the board *directs* the organization; it determines what service, product, or value is to be delivered; it identifies what population is to be served; and it establishes what ideals are to be maintained by the organization. Notice the repetition of the word *what*. Directing is about determining *what* the organization should accomplish in contrast to leading the organization on how it should accomplish the work. Both are critical, but it is the board's particular role to be dedicated to, even disciplined to, determining, clearly communicating, and ensuring the adherence of the organization to the accomplishment of that outcome—the *what* the board has set.

Directing also requires many of the same qualities in a board member that one might seek in a leader: the ability to initiate, influence, inspire, listen, and communicate. The key difference in Aligned Influence is that successful board members also have the ability to discipline themselves by limiting their activities to determining, evaluating, and planning what the organization should accomplish rather than how the organization should accomplish it. Board members understand that their own experience as leaders in other situations can be a valuable resource and support for the executive director—as long as they remain focused on the fulfillment of their distinct role as board members.

Protect Rather Than Manage

In Aligned Influence, the board protects the organization by establishing and monitoring operational boundaries that the executive is expected to respect and comply with. In doing so, the board provides boundaries within which the executive can establish operational policy and processes to ensure that the work of the organization is accomplished safely and with integrity. Board members utilize their own experience as managers to establish and monitor appropriate operational boundaries while never crossing over into the executive's role.

Like directing, the protecting role requires many of the same qualities in a board member that the executive needs to manage. Adequate business acumen and experience are essential to understand the language of financial, human resource, risk management, and compensation issues. Board members must understand the value of process, control, and documentation. They must be able to communicate in writing and interpersonally, structuring concise messages with the appropriate audience in mind. They must understand the important empowering role of a supervisor, with the ability to provide feedback and encouragement equally well. The board member must be skilled enough to manage these kinds of administrative issues, while being willing to discipline herself to her role of creating and monitoring boundaries, which allow the executive to manage well.

The board member should also understand that, even if she disagrees with a particular tactic the executive chooses, she will refrain from criticizing the choice unless it compromises one of the operational boundaries the board has established.

Enable Rather Than Accomplish

In Aligned Influence, the last role of the board is to enable the organization by advocating and assisting in resource development, which aids the executive in accomplishing the work of the organization. Board members assist in resource development by extending their personal, professional, and civic-advocacy relationships into development relationships. Therefore, a key quality of a board member is that one has significant established relationships and the ability to create more.

Relationship builders tend to be outwardly focused. They are energized by relationships and are motivated to create more. Advocacy is extended to resource development by being sensitive to an alignment between the needs and opportunities of the organization with the talents and resources of those with whom the board member has relationships. The successful board member will be genuinely interested in, even passionate about, enabling the organization to accomplish its mission. He will proactively seek out the needs and opportunities of the organization, and the talents and resources of those with whom they have relationships. Board members with this quality perceive everyone to be a winner when such an alignment is discovered.

It is at this point in the discussion that I usually get the question, "Why haven't you reminded us that the key quality in a board member is that he or she meet some level of personal financial support for the organization?" In other words, the best board member is the person who can help fund the organization. Is this true?

I realize that many boards choose board members because of their ability to provide financial resources to the organization. While it may be the happy circumstance that someone who has the ability to provide significant resources also excels at directing, protecting, and enabling the organization, in many cases that is not true. Moreover, such organizations end up burdened with a board of directors that write checks but do little else to enable the organization to accomplish its mission.

Money matters, but organizations need far more resources than just funds. Fulfilling the enabling role of board members in Aligned Influence will align much needed resources—finances, people, links to other organizations and industries, media relations, research, and so much more. In effect, the enabling role has the potential to drive more money and other resources to an organization than a board member could supply by simply writing checks. This will help organizations thrive far better and far longer than they would otherwise.

Additional Factors

Along with these qualifications for board members, you may want to include others specific to the nature of your organization. For example, if you are planning an organization centered in the field of technology, you may want to have board members who have some key understanding of various facets of that industry and its role in various sectors of local, state, national, and even worldwide communities, businesses, and the like. You may also have qualifications related to a candidate's character and reputation, ability to "play well" with others, leadership skills, trustworthiness, and so on. Whichever qualifications you compile and post, you will want to ensure that the Aligned Influence roles of directing, protecting, and enabling remain at center stage when selecting board members.

So where will you find such people? Where other business people are gathered socially. Attend community leadership meetings, chamber of commerce meetings, and civic-leadership meetings. Tell everyone you know that you are looking for high-quality people. You will be surprised how many referrals you get. The right individuals will be intrigued when you tell them that you are looking for a few good people who can inspire, initiate, influence, communicate, build relationships, and passionately enable the mission of your organization. And you will attract these people by having your own organizational house in order. They will not be satisfied sitting through an unorganized, disjointed board meeting. They will be looking for a place where they can make a difference. And you will offer them that opportunity with clearly defined roles and a clearly defined and organized set of board policies, processes, calendars, and agendas. Once you have a few of these new breed of board members, you will notice that their relationships will attract others with the same qualities to your board.

Before moving on to the executive director position, I would like to speak to the matter of passion. Previous board models have emphasized passion as a qualification for a board member. For someone to serve on a board, that individual should be passionate about the organization's mission and work. The greater the person's passion, the greater the likelihood that he or she could be an excellent board candidate.

While it's true that passion can be an indicator of someone's willingness to give up some of their time to serve on a board, it should not be among the most important qualifications for candidacy. Passion, you see, is a two-edged sword. Passion for the organization and its work is good, but too much passion can end up clouding one's objectivity as well as make it more of a struggle to remain disciplined to one's board role. Every strength becomes a weakness under certain conditions. And passion is one of those characteristics that can sometimes blind someone to seriously consider viable but difficult solutions or lead someone to get more heavily involved in ways that may be more detrimental than beneficial.

Of course, no organization wants a lukewarm or even cold board member. We want people at the top who care about what happens and want to do all they can to see our organization thrive. But under Aligned Influence, one's passion needs to be rightly channeled through directing, protecting, and enabling and not lead one to drop down into the executive director's roles and responsibilities.

Choosing the Executive Director

As we found in our discussion about board members, we will find in the approach for choosing potential executives. The approach is similar. You will want to search for candidates who have the ability to understand and implement the roles of leading, managing, and accomplishing, and staying committed to those roles. You will want to find candidates who can lead without directing, manage without protecting, and accomplish without enabling. While the best prospective executives will have the ability to set direction, establish boundaries, and advocate for the organization, they must choose to restrict themselves to the roles Aligned Influence has assigned to them.

Lead Rather Than Direct

In Aligned Influence, executives *lead* their organization by planning for how the organization's tactics, methods, and efforts need to change as the environment in which it operates changes. While the board is focused on the future of *what* the organization should accomplish, the executive is focused on *how* the organization will accomplish those goals. Through engagement with the clients the organization serves and partnering with other organizations in the community that assist it, the executive considers changes to the way the organization approaches its work. It is not the executive's role to establish what the organization will do; this is set by the board. So whoever fills the executive position needs to work within the what that the board has established.

Of course, executives who lead need to have other quality traits and skills as well. They need to be able to influence people to follow them, which requires such skills as inspiring, encouraging, challenging, listening, communicating clearly and persuasively, and casting vision, to name but a few.

Manage Rather Than Protect

Along with leading, the Aligned Influence approach views executives as *managing*. In this role, executives ensure that all of the day-to-day tasks and responsibilities are completed and that sufficient policies, procedures, training, and supervision are in place. Executives also need to ensure that sufficient documentation and structure exist for the organization's operational tasks to be completed and done so consistently over time. The role of leadership also introduces needed change, and the role of management controls change so that clients continue to be reliably served.

Also, in this role, the executive should be able to respect and comply with the protections that the board has established. In this way, the executive takes the board's boundaries and finds ways to work within them and fulfill them. Executives provide the *how* for organizational safety and integrity, while boards supply the *what* that is to be protected. As long as the executive director and his staff work within the board's protection statements, they are fulfilling the role of managing those boundaries.

The right executive, then, is the person who has the traits and experience needed to effectively fulfill this managerial role.

Accomplish Rather Than Enable

Aligned Influence also sees the executive charged with *accomplishing* the work of the organization. This requires that executives have a clear understanding of the work defined by the board and utilize the board's enabling influence to ensure that the appropriate product, service, or value is delivered. Leadership and management are both directional; they do not exist for their own sake. They exist in order to ensure that the work of the organization is appropriate and accomplished. As odd as it may sound, some executives can get so caught up in the activities of leadership and management that they lose their focus on why they work so hard on those activities. *Accomplishing* means that the executive keeps himself focused on the ultimate work of the organization, ensuring that he, his staff, and their volunteers remain aligned with accomplishing that which the board has directed them to do.

Furthermore, in Aligned Influence, the one at the top who leads the organization needs to understand and be able to work within and even improve the ecosystem of his organization. Effective leadership is not only top down but down up and even middle up and middle down. Influencers are present throughout an organization, regardless of their job title or responsibilities. And they impact those above them, below them, and around them. A good executive will do what it takes to discover these influencers and marshal their abilities to help move the organization forward in accomplishing the work.

Executive directors have enough to do attempting to fulfill these three critical roles of leading, managing, and accomplishing. Some may have occasional opportunities to seek needed resources that could help move the organization forward. But when executives can speak to their board members, share the needs the organization has, and then count on board members to fulfill their enablement role, they will discover greater freedom, energy, and time to accomplish their defined and expected roles under Aligned Influence.

Miscellaneous Matters

For the chief executive, you may have other qualifications in mind that need to be fulfilled—qualifications related to the nature of your organization and the candidate's character, reputation, level of experience, and so on, but the Aligned Influence focus on the distinct roles of chief executives will need to stand as primary.

Also, when it comes to hiring or recruiting, the ideal is that the board be in place first, and then the board should pursue the executive needed to run the organization. Once the executive director is in place, he or she is then responsible to hire or recruit whoever is needed to co-accomplish the work of the organization.

I am using the words *hire* and *recruit* intentionally. By *hire* I am referring to bringing in someone to fill a paid position. By *recruit* I am indicating seeking someone to fill an unpaid volunteer position. And notice that I used both words when talking about securing board members or executives. While it is US law that the board members of nonprofits are not to be paid, this is not the case with for-profits. Board members overseeing for-profit organizations can be paid or unpaid.

There's a common perspective, especially among nonprofits, that sees board positions as volunteer and staff positions as paid. This view has especially led start-up and small organizations to conclude that since they do not have the money to hire an executive, they must do the work of the organization. This approach, of course, rules out the option of such an organization embracing the Aligned Influence model. This is a mistake. Money should not be the determining factor for accepting Aligned Influence or from building on the Aligned Influence model from the very start. An organization will have a much cleaner start and more successful future if it recognizes and maintains the distinct yet complementary roles of the board and the chief executive while also understanding the ecosystem of the organization—as it now exists and how it could become if better led and managed.

Furthermore, it is far better for a board to refuse to adopt the roles of the executive and choose instead to stay within its own essential roles. A board that tries to perform executive roles while striving to fill its board roles is doomed to sacrifice oversight and effectiveness in at least some of its functions and responsibilities. Directing will fall prey to managing. Enabling will falter while the accomplishing role becomes all-consuming. Eventually the day-to-day concerns will become the board's focus, and no one will be left to ensure that the organization is protected, that it is going in the direction that it should be, and that it has the needed resources to get there.

It is best for organizations, no matter how small they begin, to launch themselves on the Aligned Influence foundation. If Aligned Influence is the better way to go for organizations with the complexity of a board and executive director, it is the better way regardless of the organization's age, available capital, financial structure, abilities, focus, reach, size, or for-profit or nonprofit status. Moreover, under Aligned Influence, board members can be paid or not, and executives can be paid or not. This is solely the decision of the organization's board and what the law mandates. What matters most is that whoever serves on the board and whoever serves at the executive level share the same commitment to and understanding of their distinct and essential roles and responsibilities under Aligned Influence. So when organizations seek to fill board or executive positions, they need to ask if the position will be one of directing, protecting, and enabling, or if it will fall into leading, managing, or accomplishing. Answering this question is first and foremost. Deciding whether the position is to be for pay or volunteer can come later.

Another issue organizations have with filling positions concerns what they are looking for in their selection of a chief executive. Board members are often conflicted, and they frequently have a difficult time putting words around what exactly they hope to find in an executive to lead the organization. To better guide this search, it is helpful to encourage search committees to think of the matter this way. There are two major types of skill sets— programmatic and administrative.

Programmatic skills are those that have to do with a given vocational area. For example, in education, programmatic skills would be academic and pedagogical. The ability to conduct research, develop curriculum, teach students, manage a classroom, work within an established classroom budget, and the like would be examples of the abilities included in this skill set.

In a church looking for a lead pastor, programmatic skills would be pastoral in nature: for example, the ability to preach; to study, teach, and apply Scripture; to comfort those who grieve; to conduct hospital visitations for those who are sick; to perform and explain the required religious rituals; and to introduce other people to the faith. The skills required for a town manager would include a sufficient understanding of the federal, state, and local laws and policies that bear upon his ability to perform his job. An information technology director would need to grasp the basics of technology and information science, data security, and the laws around those subjects and their application.

Administrative skills are quite different from programmatic ones. Administrative skills are integrated business-leadership skills. Individuals who have such skills understand the integrated areas of the given industry, business, ministry, civic organization, or whatever they are in. They see the big picture as well as how all the organizational parts fit together: administration, finance, human resources, marketing, sales, publicity, research, operations, and risk management. They know how to lead, manage, and inspire others, and provide vision and the general outlines of the pathway for attaining that vision. They can plan for the present and the future. People with such skills are typically not the ones who actually keep the books, make the product, sell the goods, or write the human resources policies. Their skill set is best utilized in other ways.

When organizations pursue an executive director or its equivalent, some seek a person with programmatic skills while others seek someone with administrative skills. Churches, for example, tend to hire a senior pastor who has programmatic skills—someone with pastoral abilities, such as preaching, teaching, visitation, worship, and comforting skills. With that person in place, churches may then seek to find someone with administrative skills who can support the senior pastor in his or her pastoral role. This support pastor—sometimes called the pastoral director, executive pastor, or pastor of administration—typically handles the kinds of tasks an administrator in another organization would. These are responsibilities involving human resources, finance, office management, information technology, facilities and equipment management, security, and the other sides of operations. Other pastors hired may even come under the management of the administrative pastor.

Other organizations seek an executive with administrative skills. Schools, for example, tend to hire executives with integrated business-leadership skills. They want principals, administrators, headmasters, directors, and the like to understand the organizational areas they will be overseeing, to know how these areas best work together, and to know the kind of people needed to fill positions to move the school forward. These school leaders should understand budgets; city, county, state, and federal educational law; educational philosophy; and so much more for them to be able to effectively fill their roles and responsibilities. They do not need to have all the details mastered, and they will not be hired to perform the work of a teacher, academic advisor, lunchroom attendant, bookkeeper, and the like. Such programmatic roles will be filled by others.

When your organization seeks an executive director, it needs to address which set of skills it is after: administrative or programmatic. Consider, for instance, a nonprofit such as Habitat for Humanity. When the board starts looking for an executive director, they need to ask, for instance, if the best candidate is one who has built houses all of his life or who has worked in human services and knows the faces and needs of poverty up close. If so, then the board is looking for someone with programmatic skills to lead the organization. Such a person, though, would need other individuals who understand the administrative side and can serve in that capacity to support the new chief executive who lacks that skill set.

It is more common for the executive director to be hired or recruited for her administrative skills, and then that person finds others with programmatic skills to carry out the other needs of the organization. In other words, the executive director with administrative skills may or may not have a great deal of knowledge or experience in the area of human resources, but she will bring in individuals who do to handle this organizational need. The executive director may or may not have all the skills needed to build a house or to work out the finances for families who do need a home, but he can find individuals who will accomplish this work for the organization's benefit.

Sometimes one can find a super-individual—someone who actually has both sets of skills, programmatic and administrative. But such individuals are rare, and in most cases they are hired for one set of skills over the other. So whomever your organization hires or recruits to fill the executive director position, it needs to understand what that person's skill set is, and then make room for that person to bring people into the organization who can complement his skill set with other individuals who have either programmatic or administrative skills, whichever set is most needed at the time.

In short, under the Aligned Influence model, whether a staff is paid or not or board members are paid or not is not the essential issue. An organization could be made up of all volunteer board members and all volunteer staff or with even just one paid staff member. The essential issue is that those on the board dedicate themselves to directing, protecting, and enabling, and those on staff commit themselves to whatever role they play in leading, managing, and accomplishing the work of the organization. So when an organization looks to hire or recruit, they need to ask what they are looking for in candidates. Are they looking for individuals who can fulfill the board side of Aligned Influence or the executive side? Also, are they looking for individuals with administrative skills or with programmatic skills or some sort of combination of both? Aligned Influence acknowledges and supports both types of searches, and it accommodates both within the parameters of the model.

PART III

Aligned Influence–Moving Forward

14

Achieving Alignment

I live in Colorado. I can see the eastern side of the Colorado Rocky Mountains from my home. Even from my vantage point, the mountains loom large, their summits often white with snow, and their call to journey toward them and hike and climb them is constant. They promise beauty and challenge, opportunity and reward, relaxation and danger.

Close to the foothills of these mountains sits the University of Colorado at Boulder. Locals affectionately refer to it as CU. For a few years now, I have served as adjunct faculty in the university's Leeds School of Business, teaching students about business philosophy. While they feel a pull to the mountains, their university studies keep them quite busy, though many opt to do at least some of their studying in the foothills or even in higher elevations.

CU's business students have quite a mix of backgrounds, experience, and life and career goals. For the most part, they are eager to learn about the opportunities and challenges that loom ahead of them in the world of business. As I can, I teach them about what they will face and the many ways they can direct their time and energy in more effective ways. I want them to be ready to work hard and with benefit to them, their future families, and their coworkers.

At the same time, I know they will be going into small and large businesses, corporations, schools, industrial centers, and other places of employment that will promise them much but often deliver to them more frustration and confusion than clarity, more power struggles than cooperation, more tedium than creativity, more pigeon-holing than advancement, more hierarchical structures bent on exercising authority over them than on leading them through influencing them in positive ways. No one wants to work in an oppressive environment, where the sight of beautiful mountains or vast waterways or anyplace outside the office evokes longings in staff, executives, and board members to get away and perhaps one day stay away from the job they want to like but don't.

I know organizational life does not have to be this way. It can be far better—regardless where one falls on the organizational ladder, pay scale, or depth of experience.

My development of Aligned Influence and work with a diversity of organizations to implement it are my contribution to changing the less-than-rewarding environment so many have to work in today. Board members can genuinely find something of great value to do. Executives and boards can do far more than just tolerate one another or compete against one another. Staff can feel as if their ideas and other contributions are appreciated and actually matter. Organizations can thrive, not just survive. And those entering the work force can find places where they can be satisfied while finding time to enjoy activities outside work but not out of a drive to escape their job because they find it so frustrating, disheartening, and disappointing.

I know that life inside organizations can be better for all. And when it's better there, it's better for those who have a vested interest in the success of those organizations, be they stockholders, vendors, customers, or the communities within which the organizations reside.

This better organizational life—at least for those organizations with the complexity of a board and executive—can be achieved when Aligned Influence is used to order its life. The benefits are many and far-reaching:

- Clarity of purpose, roles, and responsibilities, especially at the top;
- Internal competitiveness replaced by cooperation;
- Leadership defined and practiced as influence, not lordship;
- Leadership not relegated to just the top positions but found and encouraged throughout the organization;
- The creation and maintenance of an ordered and orderly workplace where the whole benefits the parts while the parts benefit the whole;
- Interdependent relationships that complement one another, support one another, and achieve results together;
- A clearer and more effective way to protect and improve the organization while maximizing its service to others;
- A way for an organization to achieve its mission more holistically and efficiently;
- A clear and fruitful understanding of the ecosystem of influence and how to develop and marshal it to enhance and maintain the organization's health and success;
- The expansion and alignment of the roles of boards and executives for the betterment of the organization and its leadership and staff;

- An emphasis on people over policies;
- The establishment of a complementary structure for the professional development of the board and executives.

I could go on, but this list is more than enough to display what Aligned Influence can do for an organization and those who work in it.

So if Aligned Influence is to become central to your organization, what needs to happen for this to become a reality? Here is the process.

Check Your Alignment

The first stage of the process involves checking the current alignment within your organization.

Figure 1

Consider Figure 1 again, where the gears are separate. They are not connected, though it appears they could connect if they were properly aligned. Imagine that one gear represents your organization's board and the other the executive director and his team. Are your board and executives moving together in such a way that they are clearly connected in a healthy, beneficial, and effective way? Or, like these gears, do they seem to have the potential to be connected well but clearly are not?

Every organization represents an ecosystem of influence. The key is to understand how well the influence of the board and the influence of the chief executive are aligned in your organization. What the Check Your Alignment part of the process typically reveals is how misaligned the board and the executive actually are and where this is occurring and why.

Typically, the board and the executive give different and conflicting answers to several questions, including this most basic one: Who leads your organization—your board or your chief executive? For years organizations and their consultants have been evaluating and developing boards and executives in isolation from one another. Board members go to board-governance training, and executives attend leadership-development conferences and retreats. As a result, board members and executives feel as if they are doing their jobs as they should. In reality, both groups usually end up further isolated from one another and more misaligned in their roles and responsibilities than ever before.

Through a web-based survey tool, developed in partnership and powered by Newmeasures,[27] we provide organizations with a measureable way they can explore and reflect the level of their internal alignment and its effectiveness or lack thereof. This Check Your Alignment tool is based on the Aligned Influence paradigm, so it identifies the three influence roles for the board (direct, protect, and enable) and the three influence roles for the executive (lead, manage, and accomplish). The model aligns these two distinct role sets by introducing and explaining their ordered pairs of influence (directing unites with leading, protecting unites with managing, and enabling unites with accomplishing). The Check Your Alignment survey is a low-cost and high-value first step for organizations that want to get a sense of where they are developmentally and how they could target their organizational-development investments.

Get Aligned

With a greater awareness of your organization's alignment realities, you are ready to go to the next step: Get Aligned.

Figure 6

Notice in the above graphic how the gears are connected and aligned in such a way that they can move together. This is what my team and I want to do for your organization. And the Get Aligned stage of the process is designed to do precisely this.

Aligning the ecosystem of influence in your organization is a very structured, safe, and effective process. The Get Aligned engagement will involve the board of directors, the executive director, and the executive's team in a series of sessions involving exploration, document development, and coaching—all designed to better define and align key influencer roles in the organization. The Get Aligned engagement is where the foundational work of Aligned Influence is implemented. All of the board members, the executive director, and sometimes even some of the executive's direct reports engage in a series of organizational-development efforts that address both the board's governing role and the executive's operational role.

Stay Aligned

Once an organization has become aligned from the top down, it needs to maintain that alignment of its ecosystem of influence and continue to grow in its effectiveness at utilizing the benefits of that alignment.

Figure 8

The above graphic shows the alignment that occurs under the Stay Aligned step. Not only are the gears in sync, but the bar connecting them holds them together so they stay aligned.

This Stay Aligned process requires an ongoing investment and commitment by all of the key influencers in the organization. The Stay Aligned engagement ensures the board and the executive have access to the coaching and consultation services they need each year. We provide Aligned Influence professionals to fulfill this task.

Drive Effectiveness

Under Aligned Influence, board members know that their role is to direct, protect, and enable the work of the organization. Executive directors and their key staff leaders know their role is to lead, manage, and accomplish the organization's work. Board members and executives all know the importance of staying disciplined to those roles. All of this lays the foundation for becoming more effective as individual leaders, which enhances the effectiveness of their organization.

The distinctive roles of board members and executives are ordered pairs of influence that create incredible potential for increased effectiveness in key areas of the organization. For example, the union of directing and leading focuses on the future of the organization, the union of protecting and managing zeroes in on the operational aspects of the organization, and the union of enabling and accomplishing centers on their active roles in the organization. What happens at the top inevitably ripples through all the strata of an organization. What we want to achieve with an organization is what Figure 5 shows.

Figure 5

The gears at the top are aligned and linked together in such a way that they stay aligned. The gears underneath are appropriately aligned with the top gears. In time they will be linked in such a way as to strengthen the bond between them and the top two gears. The more aligned an organization becomes from the top down, the stronger the bonds will become between all the influencers in that organization's ecosystem.

One critical way this Drive Effectiveness stage is carried out and enriched is through the discovery and development of the strengths of key influencers, especially those influencers at the top. You see, the truth is that each board member and executive team member comes "wired" or "equipped" to be better at one or more of their three distinct roles. Not all executives who manage well can lead well. And not all board members who direct well can also enable well. We all have strengths and weaknesses, wonderful talents and frustrating limitations. At Aligned Influence, we favor the strengths-based approach to leadership. Development in this area requires an exploration of each person's strengths (their wiring or talents), developing strategies to use their strengths, recruiting others who can assist them in areas that are not their strengths, and watching "game film" together over time. Watching game film involves processing with board members and executives how the mechanics of the relationship between them are actually working and how they can improve that relationship.

This type of development for key board members and executive team members can be a strategic investment for maturing organizations. In fact, what they learn about themselves will help them work with others in identifying and better utilizing their strengths in the organization. Our Aligned Influence professionals provide this discovery and coaching work for individual board members and executives.

Check your alignment.
Get aligned.
Stay aligned.
Drive effectiveness.

These four action steps operationalize the six key words of Aligned Influence no matter an organization's size, age, financial ledger, stock options, mission, stakeholders, or virtually any other characteristic. They also show executives how they can operate their organization with clear goals, protective boundaries, and appropriate board support. And they show board members how they can govern their organization in a structured manner of alignment that also gives them time to be more outward focused.

If your organization has the complexity of a board and an executive, Aligned Influence can help transform it, deepen it, broaden it, enrich it, protect it, and make it more sustainable, healthy, and effective.

15

No Matter the Organization

ligned Influence works. And it applies to any organization
that has the complexity of a board of directors and an
executive director. It doesn't matter if the organization is
a corporate or civic one, publicly held or privately owned. If it is
required to have a board along with an executive director, then
Aligned Influence applies to it and will benefit it.

Because organizations with boards can be so different, you
may still wonder if Aligned Influence really can work for your
organization. I know it can, and the reason for this begins with
what your organization has in common with all other organizations
that have boards.

Common Characteristics and Challenges

Nonprofits and publicly held for-profit corporations are
required to have boards. The same is true for almost all civic
organizations. As dissimilar as these types of organizations are,
they are still similar enough to require boards.

Investors and Investments

What, then, is this commonality? They all have investors, and the interest of the investors must be protected. Moreover, these organizations owe a return on their investors' investments. In other words, all of these organizations are managing someone else's money. All take money from others, and in doing so, they communicate the intention to provide some return to those who have provided their funds. The return on investment that is expected may differ from group to group and from individual to individual, but all of them expect a return of some kind.

The nonprofit's investors are called donors, and donors expect some value to be created in their community, country, or world.

The publicly held for-profit's investors are called shareholders, and shareholders expect a monetary return on their investment.

The civic organization's investors are called taxpayers, and taxpayers expect the efficient allocation of resources to services that the marketplace will not appropriately produce or distribute.

In these three types of organizations, boards have the responsibility to protect investor dollars and uphold investor confidence. While many organizations have definitely done both, others have failed, sometimes miserably and catastrophically. Consider first publicly held for-profit organizations. Sarbanes-Oxley and Dodd-Frank are clear reactions to the failure of the boards of some of these organizations to protect their investors. After even a quick read of both bills, one can clearly see that they are providing the kind of protection that Aligned Influence describes in the board's role to protect.

Over the last several years, there have been calls for the government to roll back the corporate legislation that was implemented in the era of Sarbanes-Oxley and Dodd-Frank. But without the framework of Aligned Influence, any rollback would simply expose investors to the same harm against which it was intended to protect them. With Aligned Influence, the government can agree to roll back legislation safely as soon as corporations implement their own governance structures that are robust enough to protect their investors.

Likewise, municipal governing boards or councils are commonly in the news for getting bogged down in operational issues that cause major battles among members. Other times, the board and council failures seem to be related to corruption often facilitated by a lack of separation of duties—say between a "strong mayor" and one or more council members—a problem that also plagues for-profit corporations that display competitions for power between executives and other board members.

Nonprofits have not been immune to failures in governance either. Their failures, which are almost always the result of misalignment and ineffectiveness, hit their investors harder than others. Donors are voluntarily investing in the production of some good that they believe will benefit others rather than themselves. As such, the trust these donors place in an organization is easily damaged by such failures. The damage can even have the collateral impact of causing donors to distrust other nonprofits in the future.

No matter the organization, boards have been identified as key to protecting the interests of those whose money they manage. But some boards have failed to protect their investors.

It is also critical that these organizations know their investors and the return that they expect. Investors are just some of your organization's stakeholders. If your organization identifies investors as their only stakeholders—or as the only ones that really matter—this will cause the board, the executive, and the rest of your organization to make choices that are not informed by all its stakeholders.

So does Aligned Influence apply to your organization and your situation? Absolutely it does. Alignment always comes before effectiveness, and effectiveness is the precursor to return on investment. If you have a board of directors, you have investors. If you have investors, you have a duty to deliver a return on their investment. It does not matter whether your investors are shareholders, donors, or taxpayers. They all expect you to manage their money wisely. And a thoroughly aligned organization is foundational to all of this.

Relationships—External and Internal

Another common feature and issue among organizations that have boards revolves around all the relationships they have to manage—relationships internal to them and, more importantly, external to them.

Relationships *internal* to an organization must be carefully structured and managed to ensure that the board is disciplined to a role that properly aligns with the executive director and his or her staff. Misalignment always leads to ineffectiveness, and ineffectiveness always harms investors' return on their investment.

Relationships *external* to an organization consist of various stakeholder groups, and these can provide tremendous input when planning for the future of an organization or evaluating its current direction. Here is yet another opportunity for alignment to occur and drive effectiveness in the work of the board and the executive director. Lack of alignment here will leave some opportunities on the table, thereby depriving the organization of all it could become and achieve. For example, when the board and executive are misaligned, they spend much more time and energy working on managing or overcoming their poor alignment than they do focusing on the mission and work of their organization. This inward conflict leaves on the table opportunities to expose the organization's work to investors and open up even more resources of support and advancement.

Now alignment is about identifying unique roles and then aligning those roles. That is the essence of Aligned Influence: three roles for the board of directors and three roles for the executive director and his or her staff. Each set of roles is definable and alignable. Alignment structures the internal relationships, and the flow of influence emanating from the alignment structures the external relationships.

Unique Characteristics and Challenges

Of course, organizations display differences too. Can Aligned Influence handle those as well? Yes, it can.

For-Profit Publicly Held Organizations

For-profit organizations start from a historical position of overlapping the executive's and board's roles in which the chief executive is also the chairperson of the board and board members are almost always paid. As such, board members can find it harder to provide checks and balances on the executive in an unconflicted manner. It was, in part, this lack of adequate checks and balances that almost unavoidably led to harm to investors and the US Congress passing legislation such as Sarbanes-Oxley and Dodd-Frank. Unfortunately, this "solution" has placed the government in the role of providing the protective role that the board was originally designed to supply.

In response, Aligned Influence provides for the separation of the executive and board chair roles that the pressure from the federal government has been incentivizing. When these roles are separated, these key corporate influencers will be faced with the same need for alignment that all other organizations required to have boards face. Aligned Influence provides a framework to achieve this alignment, which will also lead to greater organizational effectiveness.

Nonprofit Organizations

Nonprofits exist because in our market-driven economy, the market will not solve all socioeconomic issues, such as food and housing insecurity. Given such concerns, the government provides tax-exempt, tax-deductible, and tax-credit options to encourage nonprofit organizations to address these issues.

Unlike for-profits, board members of nonprofits cannot be paid for their service. Therefore, they must be recruited through their personal passion for the issue that the organization addresses and an understanding of their potential to help address that issue. It's that very passion that, while a strength, can also become an obstacle. Passionate individuals join the board because they want to solve the problem, which is fine and good, but this same passion often leads them to actions outside the board's role. They tend to be successful business leaders who, in every other area of their life, are responsible for accomplishing, and they naturally expect that they have been selected to do the same thing for the nonprofit they now serve as board members. In addition, nonprofits begin with the legacy of Policy Governance, which intends policy as the ultimate solution and which they know from previous experience does not fully work.

In contrast, Aligned Influence provides board members with well-defined, unique roles that provide the new role of enablement for them. This new role differs from and yet is aligned with the accomplishing role of the executive director and his or her team. In Policy Governance, on the other hand, board members are instructed to stay out of the work of the executive director because that is none of their business. But under Aligned Influence, board members are disciplined to a role that is different from the executive director but in a way that keeps the executive's role completely known and visible to them. No mystery exists between the board and the executive—just transparency and alignment. In addition, the board now has a clear "to-do" role—enabling the work of the organization through advocacy—which directs their energy and professional skills in an aligned and effective manner.

Of course, you can find a wide variety of nonprofits. Does Aligned Influence apply to all of those that have a board? Yes. And to show this, I'll point to independent schools, churches, and municipalities—a highly diverse lot and yet all benefitting from what Aligned Influence offers.

Independent Schools

There are many types of independent schools. Some are faith-based and intend to provide education in a context that allows them to include faith-specific instruction that would not be allowed in a public school. Some are achievement oriented, intending to provide advanced preparation for higher education. Some schools include a structure of discipline that the attending families believe will benefit students' education and life goals. Some schools exist to address significant cognitive, behavioral, or physical challenges their students face. Whatever the focus, independent schools usually provide at least some educational services that public schools generally do not offer. As such, independent schools carry the burden of delivering an educational environment and focus that are not covered by their clients' taxes. Clients pay above and beyond for an education that they believe they would not receive in an acceptable form from the public school system.

By their very nature, independent schools have a very interested client community in the form of parents. These parents view their school almost as a membership association where the membership feels like they run the association. Independent schools and membership associations act as nonprofits; therefore, they are required to have a board of directors.

Schools almost always have some kind of accrediting organization that provides a third-party credentialing of their internal structures and the quality of their work. Governance is almost always one of the structures to be assessed.

Often, independent schools are founded by a passionate person, a group of concerned parents, a church dedicated to education, or some other passion-driven organization or group. These fervent founders often have a hard time when their school starts to grow beyond their influence. These founders are clearly stakeholders, but sometimes they see themselves as the only stakeholders, or at least as the most important ones.

Aligned Influence provides independent schools with a framework that addresses the board, the head of the school, and *all* of the stakeholders, including parents (the membership), founding entities, and all other community stakeholders that are sometimes forgotten or left unacknowledged. Aligned Influence structures roles for the board members that align with the head of the school, and this model just as importantly focuses their attention on all stakeholders. Through Aligned Influence, board members who are also parents have a better way of separating their parental role from their board role and gain a way to better explain that difference to other parents. Accrediting organizations almost always give Aligned Influence boards commendations for excellence in governance, and the Check Alignment assessment gives these boards an empirical approach to the self-assessment portion of every accreditation visit.

Churches

At their core, churches are faith-based membership organizations that are both places of worship and registered nonprofit corporations. Consequently, they have at least two sources of input about the role and structure of their board of directors: their theological text (the Bible) and corporate best practices. Seminaries typically provide very little guidance to students and church leaders about church governance. So leaders tend to try to gather all of their guidance from the Bible or adopt governance strategies that they see in their community. Some churches that have strong denominational ties get a governance structure dictated to them from their denomination's headquarters.

Regardless of where churches get their guidance, they have seen the same kinds of governance failures that the secular world has experienced. The leaders of very large churches are often charismatic leaders[28] who sometimes unintentionally restrict the kind of balanced influence that both their theological texts and corporate best practices advocate. Instead, what they say goes, and what they receive from fellow church leaders and their congregations tends to provide little oversight.

Aligned Influence, on the other hand, provides corporate best practices that align well with the key leadership/influencer roles identified in the biblical books of 1 Timothy and Titus. Overseer (elder) and servant leader (deacon) roles clearly align with the board and executive roles as outlined in the Christian Scriptures. In fact, churches that have implemented Aligned Influence have discovered additional organizational benefits from more clearly defining and aligning these biblical roles.

Municipalities

Cities and towns are not corporations, but as civic organizations established by or allowed to be established by state statute, they too are required to have oversight groups, which are often called councils or trustees. These overseers are almost always elected rather than selected or appointed. As such, candidates for elected offices frequently run campaigns on platforms that tout solving big problems in the community. In other words, they run on a ticket that advocates accomplishing and leading—roles under Aligned Influence that are for the executive to do, not for the board. This leads candidates (and those who vote for them) to confuse their civic roles with those of the town or city manager, who are, in fact, serving in the executive role.

In fact, in some municipalities with so-called "strong mayor" models, the same problem that has plagued for-profit corporations surfaces: the mayor is also the city manager. In these situations, municipalities have decided that the way to address the alignment between the two roles is to eliminate the need for alignment. They place the executive gear over the board gear and think that this overlap of roles and functions will actually serve their communities better. In effect, however, this governing approach greatly diminishes the checks and balances for which the oversight council was established. And it promotes destructive competitions for power that undermine the municipality's ability to serve all of its stakeholders fairly and justly.

Another way the damaging effects of the lack of alignment shows up is when councils use a policy set incorrectly. For instance, by statute, councils are almost always required to approve municipal codes before they go into effect. This statutory requirement was clearly established to ensure that the municipal codes were in the best interests of citizens. But by approving them all, councils sometimes begin to mistake the codes designed to operate the municipality as their governance policies. Consequently, councils start inserting themselves into situations that are properly in the domain of the city manager, and this creates frustration and generates unnecessary power plays as it further confuses the roles of the council and the city manager.

In contrast, Aligned Influence observes that there are three sets of policies in a mature organization: those that are used to establish the organization, those that are used to govern it, and those that are used to operate it. Municipal boards benefit from understanding that the first two are clearly their concern, and that although they are required to review and approve everything that appears in the third set, it is clearly the document set that the city manager uses to accomplish the work of the community under his purview.

Aligned Influence clearly informs elected officials what their role really is and how it is aligned to the role of the city manager. This clarity has provided councils who have adopted Aligned Influence with better ways of addressing the issues that developers and other economic actors bring to them.

The Bottom Line

So then, does Aligned Influence apply to your organization? As long as it has a board and executive director, then yes, it does.

The intent of this book has been to explore some history of governance, to make clear observations about and connections to what we have learned about governance over the years, and to propose a new and much better way forward. In effect, Aligned Influence presents a new, revolutionary paradigm in organizational leadership structure. This is a paradigm that has proven its applicability and effectiveness across all types of organizations that have the complexity of a board of directors and an executive team. For-profit, nonprofit, civic, corporate, faith-based, secular. No matter the organization, if it has a board and executive, Aligned Influence speaks into it and will benefit it.

Remember, effectiveness always follows alignment; it never happens the other way around.

Alignment matters. It always has. We just haven't always given alignment all that it's due. Aligned Influence finally does this.

For organizations new or old, Aligned Influence is the best way to achieve the alignment needed to obtain and secure, for many years of changes to come, the protections you need and the successes you seek for your organization. You and your organization can protect your investors' interests while making significant differences in your community and your world. Aligned Influence is designed to help you do that incredibly beneficial and rewarding work.

ACKNOWLEDGMENTS

My work at Aligned Influence has been fueled and encouraged by a number of colleagues and friends. This book specifically has been made possible by Bill Watkins. Bill is the founder and president of Literary Solutions. While working with him, I learned very quickly that writing a book is vastly different from writing a series of white papers. Bill was able to take my content and form it into this book. It was exciting for me to see the impact this material had on his life and how, at times, we sharpened each other through the writing process. Thanks, Bill, for all you gave to this project.

ABOUT THE AUTHOR

Ken Schuetz is the CEO and founder of Aligned Influence Consulting and the creator of the Aligned Influence model. Ken invested the first twenty-five years of his career as an executive at the University of Colorado in Boulder, Colorado, where he also earned his degree and currently is a member of the adjunct faculty of the Leeds School of Business. Ken is the author of many articles. He has served on the boards of schools, churches, and nonprofits and as the chairman of the Substantial Services Taskforce for the National Education Broadband Service Association and the International Development Committee for St. Vrain Valley Habitat for Humanity.

Ken utilizes his years of experience as an executive in higher education, his multiple years in board leadership, and his academic background in organizational communication to help organizations achieve the effectiveness they and their communities of interest desire. His work in organizational leadership has extended to many organizations across the United States: for-profit, nonprofit, faith-based, and secular.

For more about Ken Schuetz and Aligned Influence Consulting, go to www.alignedinfluence.com.

ENDNOTES

1   Franklin A. Gevurtz, "The Historical and Political Origins of the Corporate Board of Directors," *Hofstra Law Review*, vol. 33, no. 1, art. 3, see especially pp. 154–66.

2   See, for example, John Carver, *Boards That Make a Difference: A New Design for Leadership in Nonprofit and Public Organizations*, 3rd ed. (San Francisco, CA: Jossey-Bass, 2006).

3   These white papers, as well as many additional ones, can be found on my website www.AlignedInfluence.com.

4   David Emerson, executive director, Habitat for Humanity of the St. Vrain Valley, Colorado, video interview, https://www.youtube.com/watch?time_continue=46&v=bRXmHeW8skc.

5   Jeff Durbin, town manager of Frazer, Colorado, video presentation, https://www.youtube.com/watch?v=_gm-jnJ37FO0&t=0s&list=PLj2mWZC1I9DR_C4EN-HsP76g-BwJ8P76Ov&index=14; https://www.youtube.com/watch?v=o3zZd0pM4nw&list=PLj2mWZC1I9DR_C4ENHsP76g-Bw-J8P76Ov&index=14.

6   "CharityWatch Hall of Shame" (October 2013), Charity Watch, http://www.charitywatch.org/articles/CharityWatchHallof-Shame.html.

7   "Notable Nonprofit Executive Spending Scandals," *Dallas Morning News* (April 29, 2012), http://www.dallasnews.com/investigations/headlines/20120429-notable-nonprofit-executive-spending-scandals.ece.

8   Richard Leblanc and James Gillies, *Inside the Boardroom: How Boards Really Work and the Coming Revolution in Corporate Governance* (Mississauga, Canada: John Wiley & Sons, 2005), 10–11.

9   Ibid., 11.

10   Sometimes, of course, government takes the wrong action and some of the citizenry rise up in protest and lead the way of change.

11   Will Kenton, "Dodd-Frank Wall Street Reform and Consumer Protection Act," *Investopedia*, May 10, 2019, https://www.investopedia.com/terms/d/dodd-frank-financial-regulatory-reform-bill.asp.

12   Kayla Gillan, "Sarbanes-Oxley Has Enhanced Investor Protection," *New York Times* (July 24, 2012), http://www.nytimes.com/roomfordebate/2012/07/24/has-sarbanes-oxley-failed/sarbanes-oxley-has-enhanced-investor-protection.

13   Franklin A. Gevurtz, in his essay "The Historical and Political Origins of the Corporate Board of Directors," *Hofstra Law Review*, vol. 33, no. 1, art. 3, shows that boards were established for at least four core reasons: (1) a belief that group decisions were generally more reliable than the decisions of a single individual; (2) a commitment to the principle that decisions that affect the entire group should be approved by the group or the group's representatives; (3) the need for representatives of the group to adjudicate disputes arising from its members; and (4) to provide a means to protect the investments of shareholders and stakeholders. In contemporary times, I find this fourth reason to be the most definitive one for establishing a board.

14   Brock Romanek, "Sarbanes-Oxley Was a Good Step, but There

Are Miles to Go," *New York Times* (July 24, 2012), http://www.nytimes.com/roomfordebate/2012/07/24/has-sarbanes-oxley-failed/sarbanes-oxley-was-a-good-step-but-there-are-miles-to-go.

15   For evaluations of Carver's Policy Governance model as well as the many other contemporary models, see: "The Policy Governance Model: A Critical Examination," by Alan Hough (July 2002), paper published by the Centre of Philanthropy and Nonprofit Studies at Queensland University of Technology, Brisbane, Australia, https://www.academia.edu/272744/The_Policy_Governance_model_a_critical_examination; "Models of Corporate / Board Governance," *Leadership Acumen*, issue 21, http://www.banffexeclead.com/AcumenPDF/Governance%20Articles/Leadership%20Acumen%2021%20V10%20Models%20of%20Corporate%20&%20Board%20Governance.pdf; and "Theorizing about Board Governance of Nonprofit Organizations: Surveying the Landscape," by Alan Hough, Myles McGregor-Lowndes, and Christine Ryan (Brisbane, Australia: Queensland University of Technology), paper presented at the 34th annual conference of the Association for Research on Nonprofit Organizations and Voluntary Action (Nov. 17–19, 2005).

16   Carver, *Boards That Make a Difference*, chap. 3.

17   Ibid., xiii-xv.

18   Alan Hall, "'I'm Outta Here!' Why 2 Million Americans Quit Every Month (and 5 Steps to Turn the Epidemic Around)," *Forbes* (March 11, 2013), http://www.forbes.com/sites/alanhall/2013/03/11/im-outta-here-why-2-million-americans-quit-every-month-and-5-steps-to-turn-the-epidemic-around/.

19   John C. Maxwell, *The 21 Irrefutable Laws of Leadership: Follow Them and People Will Follow You*, revised and updated ed. (Nashville, TN: Thomas Nelson, 2007), 11, 13.

20   This insight regarding order and disorder is built in part on St. Augustine's thought regarding the ontological primacy of goodness over evil, of moral order over disorder. See his work *The Enchiridion on Faith,*

Hope, and Love, 10–12.

21   The Deming Institute, "Deming the Man—Timeline," from the 1982 entry, https://www.deming.org/theman/timeline.

22   "Chapter 2: W. Edwards Deming's Theory of Management," slide 11, cbapp.csudh.edu/depts/finance/frezayat/.../PPlectures/Chapter%202.pp.

23   See Garrett Hardin, "The Tragedy of the Commons," *Science* 162 (1968): 1243–48, http://www.autoteiledirekt.de/science/tragedia-usuniecia-garrett-hardin-1968.

24   Each of these examples was inspired by Thayer Watkins, "Suboptimization," the San José State University Economics Department, http://www.sjsu.edu/faculty/watkins/suboptimum.htm.

25   Jeff King, interview with Ken Schuetz, posted on YouTube.com, August 23, 2015, https://www.youtube.com/watch?v=K6e91illYJw&list=PLj2mWZC1I9DR_C4ENHsP76g-BwJ8P76Ov&index=8.

26   Harold Tessendorf, interview with Ken Schuetz, posted on YouTube.com, August 9, 2015, https://www.youtube.com/watch?v=0t1V_r8R8XM&list=PLj2mWZC1I9DR_C4ENHsP76g-BwJ8P76Ov&index=1.

27   See www.newmeasures.com for more information on this company.

28   Here "charismatic leaders" does not necessarily designate leaders of a Pentecostal persuasion. Rather, I use this phrase to refer to church leaders who inspire in others the desire to follow them and their teaching sometimes even irrespective of the leaders' theological commitments or denominational ties. These are leaders who others find personally appealing, alluring, fascinating, welcoming, and even captivating.

Printed in the USA
CPSIA information can be obtained
at www.ICGtesting.com
JSHW022326140824
68134JS00019B/1314